The Yamaguchi Manuscripts

An Epic Apparent Economic Allegory
(AEAEA)

—w—

Rands

Coulson

DEDICATION

To those over the millennia that have suffered the effects of debasement at the hands of monarchs, rulers and central bankers.

CONTENTS

Preface   vii

Part One

I   Caveman Economics   1
II   Value   5
III   What is Money?   9
IV   Governments   15
V   A Change of Money   20
VI   Banks   28
VII   Shares   38
VIII   Bonds   43
IX   Inflation   49
X   Central Banks   55
XI   Stock Markets & Futures Contracts   63
XII   From Gold Standard to Fiat   73
XIII   The Great Divergence   81
XIV   PWOS-NOM-FOR   86
XV   Post PWOS-NOM-FOR   95
XVI   Rise of the Crimsons   103
XVII   The Great Pleasure Boat Bubble   112
XVIII   The Fallout and the Aftermath   122

Part Two

I   The State of the World   130
II   The DUMBFUCS   143
III   The Island   150
IV   The Crimsons   163
V   The Valley   178
    Afterword   191
    Appendix – Acronymology   192
    Abbreviations   195
    Glossary   197

PREFACE

The two authors of this book met for the first time in Japan. One Australian, one South African, we were sent at separate times by separate companies to the small industrial enclave of Kure, close to Hiroshima. Having vastly contrasting backgrounds, one a master brewer, the other a writer, we were separately avid students of history and both drawn to the ridiculous goings on of the international financial markets.

Being close followers of the precious metals markets for many years we could not resist chasing whispers of gold in one of the local river systems. Armed only with the basic instruments of a small sluice, a pan and two shovels, we went prospecting. It was during one of these expeditions deep in the misty mountains of Yamaguchi that we were confronted by an event that would change our lives. In the shady bank of a fast flowing river, we stumbled upon a tiny cave. Not far from the entrance, under a pile of unearthly heavy stones we uncovered an earthen ceramic container. As it looked unimportant, Mike picked up one of the stones and struck it hard in the center, smashing the fragile container into pieces. Lying torn on the root covered, foul smelling cave floor were a number of parchments. We set to work interpreting them, and realized that they tell a story from a parallel reality. The tale spans multiple generations, and is set mostly in a place known only as the Valley. It's a story about the birth and death of fiscal and monetary systems, cheating governments, conniving bankers, money printing, trade wars, real wars, bubbles and bailouts, and a pathological addiction to acronyms. It is at once wildly amusing and deeply disturbing. Disturbing, because the likeness it bears to our own world is so obvious that it simply cannot be overlooked. The events in our world and theirs run parallel right up to the present moment. But we realized that this parallel reality was offset slightly ahead of our time. It must have been, because the story continues past the present day, into the future. Could it all just be a coincidence? Or could it be that these forgotten pages give us an insight into our own world, and its very near future? You'll have to decide for yourself if it's just a farce, or something much more.

PART ONE

∽ I ∼
CAVEMAN ECONOMICS

In which the unchangeable laws of human and economic nature are discovered.

In the beginning there is a single family of humans that live together in a cave. There is a mother, a father and three children. Because they are the only family, they have no need for a name. Their lives are simple, but the world is volatile, and resources are limited. Thus economics is a matter of pure survival. Except during those rare moments when they relax or have fun, all their efforts must be directed towards gaining control over, or manipulating their environment in such a way as to satisfy their needs. As such they must firstly understand what their needs are, and then figure out how best they can cater for them. Of course, the best guide to their needs are their instincts. But humans are not only driven to satisfy their immediate needs, and it is in their nature to think ahead. The human knows that if he eats all his fish today without a thought for tomorrow, he may sleep well tonight but will wake to a hunger that will give way to a slow and agonizing death. As such, he must economize. He must learn to balance his present and future needs.

The family share a bond so strong that, for the most part, we observe no noticeable conflict within the unit. Of course the mother and father shout at one another, and the children fight over who got to eat more honey covered beetles. But the parents are bound through an identical and equal investment in their children: each child, is one half them. They both recognize the other's role in ensuring the children's survival. But this realization increases the psychological torment they feel. Sometimes the father envies his long dead grandfather, the last monkey in their family line. How simple his life was, it seems. But he doesn't have time for these kind of self-indulgent thoughts, and must work hard to stay alive.

One day he notices that his eldest son has gone missing. He imagines that something awful has happened – perhaps he was eaten by a bear or a lion. He goes out looking for him, wailing in the wind, preparing for the worst. But then he notices something most unusual. His son has taken an animal skin and wrapped it around some sticks. He appears to be using it as if it were a cave.

'What have you done here?' the father asks his son.

'I took the animal skin like the ones you always throw away, and made myself a shelter. I call it the Animal Skin Shelter Device, or ASSD.'

'I see' said the father. 'And you won't be coming home to our cave then?'

'I'm afraid not' says the young man.

Although the father is sad to see his son leave, he is impressed with his ingenuity. He reports back to the family, explaining what has happened. The mother is angry and distraught, but the father reminds her that they always emphasized the importance of efficiency, and in the past the animal skins had done nothing but attract flies.

Then, two days later his next son has gone. When he goes looking for him, he is not altogether surprised to find that he too has built himself an ASSD on the edge of the riverbank. A week later his daughter vanishes and he finds her living in a spacious ASSD several meters away from her younger brother. She explains that she did not in fact build it herself. Her eldest brother built it and is letting her live in it provided she picks all his berries for him.

'But why didn't you just stay with us in the cave?' the father asks.

'Because everyone's getting an ASSD dad' she says.

He mopes back to his cave and explains the situation to his wife. She is convinced that it will not last and that soon enough the family will return. But two days later he wakes to find that she too has gone. When he finds her living in an ASSD of her own, he feels so betrayed that he returns to the cave and does not leave it for over a month.

When he finally emerges he sees along the bank an entire line of ASSDs. He counts ten in total.

'What is going on here?' he asks his wife.

'We got carried away' she says.

The younger brother had built a house for his mother, hoping that she would provide berries for him in exchange. The older brother had built another one for his sister believing that she would in turn provide him with beetles and roast flies. The sister had learnt to make ASSDs too, and she had built one for her mother out of kindness (she claims). The mother had built one for each of her sons, hoping that in exchange they would provide her with food in her old age. Each brother had built another one for himself, and one for the other, hoping to secure a constant supply of meat as repayment for the service. Each brother was

3

planning to use the meat from the other brother to pay the mother back for their respective houses.

The father's horror is magnified when he sees heaps of entrails left rotting on the banks of the river alongside large piles of festering meat. In their frenzy the family have killed all the animals in the area and now they have nothing but unnecessary ASSDs to show for it. They say that they're all very sorry and agree to return to the cave.

As we can see from this early story, the human has always been looking for ways to use things more efficiently, always been fond of acronyms, and always created bubbles.

—◦ II ◦—
VALUE

Where it is revealed that value is relative.

No one is entirely sure what happened after the ASSD bubble, and it's agreed that it's best not to ask too many questions. What we do know is that the last time we saw the valley's first family there was a mother, a father, two brothers and a sister. Now there are two families.

The family that lives on the riverbank spends most of their time fishing and have become master fishermen. In order to distinguish themselves from the other family (both firmly agree that making this distinction is important) they have taken on a common name. They are known as the Fishers. The other family have become master basket weavers and are known as the Baskets. The fruits of their labor can be said to have value because they serve the purpose of keeping them alive. This is known as use value. The fish pulled out of the river by the Fishers are a source of protein. The baskets woven by the Baskets can be used to store and carry goods. Each family relies on the other to satisfy a need that they themselves cannot or choose not to satisfy. The Fishers need the baskets to carry and store their fish and the Baskets need the fish to cater for their protein needs (though of course, they don't actually use the words 'protein needs'). To obtain each other's products they must exchange them. Each product therefore has two values: a use value and an exchange value.

In the case of the Fishers they need to pull out one fish per day on average to cater for their protein needs. Should they fail to do so they will all die. If they pull out two fish in one day, they can either eat them both and satisfy their mouths and stomachs beyond mere survival, or they can store the fish and preserve it for a day when they do not catch any fish. If they should catch a third fish in one day, we can be almost certain that unless they are struck by a desire to binge eat, they will store it. They know from experience that fishing is not reliable, and that a big catch one day does not guarantee any catch at all the next. They know from experience that if they hang fish up to dry their cave will stink. Thus they need to store them alive, in a special inlet, inside a basket. Due to the nature of the material used in the baskets they must replace them twice per month. Because of the daily fluctuations in catch size, they must ensure that they are able to store up fish in excess of those needed to satisfy their daily protein needs, and use them as items of exchange with the Basket family.

The Baskets are able to cater for the majority of their protein needs by catching and eating slow moving reptiles that come past their cave mouth. They catch them using their baskets as traps, and preserve them alive inside their cave until such time as they are needed. However, each month their protein needs are not quite met and they rely on the fish pulled out of the river by the Fishers to make up this deficit. The two families send representatives to meet each other twice a month and make exchanges. The Fishers come with their fish and the Baskets their baskets. Neither lets the other know exactly what position they are in, in terms of excess or shortage. One month one family has a greater surplus of goods and the next month it's reversed. But on average the Baskets need to get fourteen fish per month (or seven per trade) and the Fishers need two baskets per month (one per trade). There is no fixed relationship in value. Each trading session both parties are aware that should something have changed in the circumstances of the other, their produce may not have the exchange value it once did. But, as things remain in relative equilibrium, it can be said that seven fish have the trade value of one basket, and one basket has the trade value of seven fish. The value is not fixed, but at this point we can say that the trade value is stable.

One day a young Basket, a girl named Hilary, is washing her clothes in the river when she notices a medium sized fish tangled and stuck in some reeds. She runs over to try and catch it but it wriggles free. Her brain starts ticking and she runs home to her family and asks them why on earth don't they use their baskets to catch fish themselves. The way the 'so called Fishers' are doing it, with long lines of reed and hooks of stone, is ridiculously cumbersome and slow. If they use a basket and submerge it just below the surface near the edge of the river, there is every chance that they can catch all the fish they need by themselves. The father likes this idea and gives it a try. As it turns out, his young daughter Hilary is correct and the next week when the trade is set to take place, the father Billy – Billy the Bastard – as he will later be known to the Fishers – arrives with a smug look on his red face. He plays with his black moustache as Frederick Fisher approaches him with the fish and says, 'shall we make the trade: seven fish, one basket?'

But Billy Basket says, 'how about no? How does that sound, Freddy?'

He'd never before called him Freddy, and Frederick knew that something was wrong.

'Why not?' asks Frederick, while nervously scratching his upper thigh.

'Because', says Billy, 'they are worthless to me.'

He yanks his moustache unnecessarily hard and turns and walks away.

Frederick sends his son Adam to go and spy on the Baskets and the boy comes back with the disturbing news. Frederick realizes that though the fish he pulls out still have the exact same use value, their exchange value has been reduced to zero. Even if he improves his own fishing method and hauls out thousands of fish a day, they will be of no use to him in acquiring the baskets he needs for storing and carrying his produce. Neither Frederick nor anyone in his family knows how to make baskets from reeds. In the past the ability to catch fish was an economic tool: the Fishers could manipulate their environment in such a way as to cater for their protein needs and acquire items with trade value to exchange for other items that met other needs. Now, their skill has lost its use in relation to trade.

Overnight, relations between the two families have shifted dramatically. If the Fishers wish to survive they have three options: find someone else with whom they can trade, acquire something new that has trade value, or learn to make baskets and become completely self-sufficient. Should they fail to do so, there is a chance that the Fisher family will either die out, or come to rely on the charity of the Baskets. And in these early days there is no such thing as charity.

—ᔥ III ᔦ—

WHAT IS MONEY?

In which it is learned that money must have more than five inherent properties.

Our valley has grown dramatically. There are numerous families and unfamiliar faces. We have farmers and lumberjacks. Fishers have married Baskets. There are rumors of affairs. Bastard children are commonplace. There's love, hate, envy, joy: we have, in short, a society. Economics has become vastly more complex, and simple swap-style trade is becoming increasingly unviable.

Against the grain of expectation the Fishers managed to regain control of the fishing market. They found ways of adding extra value to their products by extracting the oil from the fish, and today have a near monopoly on the fish oil and fresh fish trade. However, due to natural ecological changes, the vast majority of their catch is caught during a single month in early spring when migratory fish come through the valley in their thousands. If they do not capitalize on this moment, there will not be another chance. The valley has seasonal foods, and fish is the spring dish of choice. They have no problem trading their fish in that month, and they are able to acquire vast quantities of goods in a very short space of time. But what to do with thousands of apples, bananas, grapes, potatoes, and hunks of fresh meat? They could live like kings for a month and spend eleven months as beggars. But they're a proud family, the Fishers, having suffered humiliations in the past, and so they need to come up with a solution.

The best course for the Fishers is to find a product needed by all of their fellow valley people throughout the year, and acquire as much of it as possible. The head of the family, Johnson. P. Fisher, a tall, slow walking man who fancies himself as a thinker, puts his mind to the task. After due consideration he concludes that a suitable substance needs to meet five basic requirements. It must be durable: able to survive, in a useful state, for at least the duration of a single year. It must have some inherent value. It must be divisible. It must be easy to store and easy to transport. And it must be fungible: any unit of the substance should be interchangeable with any other unit. He decides that of all the products currently available in the valley, the one that best meets these requirements, is manure. Everyone needs at least some manure and if he can get enough of it, he can certainly provide for his family year-round. And so, through shrewd but fair trading, Johnson. P. Fisher is able to build up massive reserves. One of the outhouses traditionally used as a hanging room for dry fish, is converted into a manure storeroom. Johnson is extremely pleased with himself and throws a large dinner for his family.

'Fishers' he says, 'let us propose a toast to our new found wealth and stability!'

They cheer!

But that night the youngest daughter, Sally, is unable to sleep. The smell of manure wafts in through her window and she decides that in the morning she will tell her father that his idea is a failure. But when she wakes the next day,

Johnson is standing in the kitchen, beaming from ear to ear, a large leg of lamb lying on the table.

'Swapped thirty pounds of manure for this' he says, and gives his daughter a big hug. She doesn't have the heart to break his spirits, and decides that she'll just have to get used to it.

From then on, Johnson doesn't go anywhere without a bag of manure slung over his shoulder. At first his plan seems to be a winner. Farmers are always in need of manure, and so whenever he needs some food he's able to swap out some dung. With time the family adjusts to the constant smell.

But then things start to go wrong. A boy named Jeremy Bread breaks off his engagement with Sally Fisher. He has a note delivered to her house that reads, *When she smelt like fish she was quite a dish. Now she smells like dung, and I'll have none.*

Johnson is furious and insists that Bread's family will be brought to task for their rudeness. He refuses to back down from his idea and starts walking around with pockets full of dung, trying to trade it for anything and everything. He'll walk into shops and say, 'two of those please' before slamming down a handful of manure on the counter. But shopkeepers don't take kindly to this, and more and more people refuse to trade with him, saying, 'we don't want your stinking money!'

By the time the winter comes the situation is dire and the Fishers are on the verge of starvation. Many of the farmers have all the manure they need and see no point in trading with him. Moreover the supply he has left is starting to freeze. He hacks off frozen blocks of dung and tries to trade it for anything, but nobody wants it. He cannot believe how badly his plan has failed. His daughter looks anaemic, his wife is frail. His son is forced to take a job working for the

Baskets. They give him just enough food to keep his family alive until the springtime.

When the winter ends, just before the fish run, Johnson's son Albany insists that his father add a sixth property to his 'sound money' checklist. At present his list reads:

1) Durable

2) Fungible

3) Divisible

4) Portable

5) Have inherent value

He now adds point number 6 – It must not stink!

In the spring the fish run again and Johnson and Albany haul in an impressive catch. Albany tells his father that this year he will be responsible for the trading. His father's general idea was good, but the substance he went after was a disaster. Johnson agrees to step aside

The son decides that the best substance available is not manure, but rice. Valley citizens eat rice throughout the year as a complement to their seasonal meal and there are numerous rice farmers in the valley. Through some clever trading he manages to acquire sacks full of rice that he stores in the freshly cleaned, scrubbed and sterilized outhouse.

This time the plan works. The Fishers fortunes turn around. One year they were considered smelly pariahs, the next year smart pioneers. They keep it up and time and again they are able to satisfy their needs year round using this method. Sally gets married to a man far better than Bread, and Albany is able to start up his own family. Johnson and his wife Joanna are able to live abundant lives. Other seasonal producers observe their success and are keen to adopt the method themselves. Apple farmers, grape farmers, lumberjacks, even potato farmers whose product would satisfy all their carbohydrate needs, start storing rice when they see its effectiveness in year-round trading.

Rice becomes widely referred to simply as 'money'. It is accepted as a store of wealth, but also as an advanced accounting tool. This means that it facilitates a wider number of transactions than would otherwise have been possible. For example, a banana farmer is willing to trade four bananas for one cup of rice. The banana farmer needs two cups of rice to trade for the six potatoes his family needs for dinner. To acquire half a kilogram of pork he needs three cups of rice, which requires that he sell twelve bananas. In the past he would have to have traded six bananas with the potato farmer and twelve bananas with the pig farmer. Now however, he can trade his bananas with anyone at any time for a set quantity of rice. In the past he would also have only been able to trade with someone whose wares he desired. For example, the banana farmer and his family are all allergic to nuts. Without the medium of money, no economic exchange could take place between the banana farmer and the nut farmer. Now however, the nut farmer – who is not allergic to bananas – can trade a set quantity of rice for the tasty yellow fruit.

With the introduction of money into the valley, we find ourselves coming into contact with a new theory: price. In the past, certain items or services had different values. The value of one item would fluctuate in relation to another, depending on a variety of circumstances, as seen in the example of the fish and the baskets. As the number of citizens in the valley has increased, so has the number of goods and services available. The value of something can thus be measured in relation to numerous different things. Fish can be measured against baskets, which can be measured against nuts, which can be measured against wheat against land against timber. One freshly felled tree for instance has the value of a hundred bananas, which have the value of three baskets, which have the value of twenty one fish. All of these items are now measured against one common item and their 'price' is given in cups of rice or portions thereof.

In years to come the inhabitants of the valley and those people that live in neighboring regions will become so accustomed to money, and so accustomed to its being controlled by a central governing body that they will forget that money is not invented as a concept and then imposed upon the population. It comes about naturally as a consequence of economic activity – and a product of trial and error – and as its usefulness becomes widely accepted, its position in society becomes entrenched.

As this happens a new economic phenomenon arises. If you produce more than you consume you have a means of storing your wealth over your lifetime. You can comfortably provide for your needs and for the needs of your descendants. If you can do this, and do it best, you will be the first rich man in the valley. Your wealth will be your power and you will be able to influence the economy and society as you see fit.

─◦ IV ◦─
GOVERNMENT

In which Rich discovers the unifying power of the stick.

The first rich man in the valley was – not surprisingly – a rice farmer. When he was still a teenager his father died and he took over an enormous tract of land that ran alongside the river. His position gave him an advantage over all other farmers in the Valley at that time, and he was able to grow vast amounts of rice. He was sensible enough not to exchange all of it each season, but instead store significant quantities as money. He was known during the course of his life as Uncle Rice. On his death he was given the posthumous name Mr. Rich, and his descendents have since used this as their family name. We are now in the third generation of Riches, and the current head of the family looks set to uphold an established tradition, one that has had two major consequences: an increased degree of intra-societal unity, and a vast increase in the power and wealth of the Rich family.

The system was thought up and implemented by Uncle Rice, aka Rich The First, in his golden years. His wealth had bought him time, his time he spent in observation, and his observation had led him to certain conclusions. Each family produced different goods, it was true, and their habits and

15

ways were never identical. But they all needed security; all needed water. All were happier and more productive when the roads they used to get to work on were not falling to pieces. And fires could be dealt with more effectively by a designated unit than a group of untrained fools with broken buckets. Did it not make sense therefore for each member of the valley to make a monthly contribution towards a common fund that would be used to address the aforementioned common challenges? And did it not make sense for him to be the patron of this fund, the man to whom the money came? Was he not the best and indeed only man suitable for this task? On all counts, he concluded, the answer was yes.

This was a new form of economic activity: an expansion of economics and a distortion of pure trade, because the monthly payment was involuntary. Uncle Rice believed that sometimes cooperation was best achieved through coercion.

His first task was to put up posters around the Valley: *Are you a big man who likes wielding a big stick? Are you noticeably disfigured? Do you have: missing fingers, large scars or cracked teeth? Do you have a tough name: Frank, Tony, Chuck? Then Uncle Rice has work for you.*

After selecting the most appropriate candidates, Rich I inducted the men as the valley's 'tax collectors'. He explained that the future of the valley civilization depended on their success. They would roam from house to house with the simple choice: pay or die? If a household handed over the required amount – thirty percent of their earnings – they would live. If not, they would die. Many men were hanged in the town square, and many were beaten to death. But most were more than happy to hand over their hard earned money to the enormous, disfigured, stick-bearing men. When the public was suitably afraid and intimidation no longer necessary, Rich's Goons or RGs, as they'd become known, were relieved of their duties. As they had become somewhat attached to their sticks, he transferred them instead to the newly formed traffic department, so they could direct wagons and carriages along the newly paved streets. With the success of his taxation system Uncle Rice and later his descendents became the largest employees in the valley. They employed road-workers and firemen, men to keep order and men to collect taxes. RGs that were not transferred to the traffic department, were used as guards to protect the valley. They created entertainment to keep the unhappy valley folk distracted from the mediocrity of their lives. Particularly popular were large stadiums in which the foolish citizens who chose not to pay their tax were fed to lions. Written on the large entrance halls was the phrase: *Only One Thing is Certain: Death OR Tax*. With time this phrase became distorted to death and taxes. The distorted version is in no way true to the original, but its inherent truthfulness has ensured its survival.

Of course Rich also built a large house for himself and gave important positions to his most trusted friends and allies. They too built themselves large houses and together formed an organization that became known as The Government. As taxes were constantly levied in rice, the power and status of the grain became so deeply entrenched in society that some even forgot that it could be eaten. Its exchange value so exceeded its use value, that not even a fool would consider boiling it for dinner. During the reign of Rich II, government and citizens alike began referring to the monetary system as the Rice Standard.

It was during this time that a cow farmer known as Samuel Stainbourn or Stainbourn I attempted to take power away from Rich. He had studied monetary history in great detail and came across the account of Johnson. P. Fisher's attempt to use manure as money. He believed that Fisher was a visionary and that his plan had failed only because he had had insufficient quantities of dung. He envisioned a great Dung Standard in which all citizens would choose dung over rice. In some ways Stainbourn I can be considered a visionary, for he imagined a monetary system in which the commodity money itself was not carried on the citizen's person but was rather stored in a central location. They would carry a promissory note in lieu of the actual commodity. But unfortunately he had chosen the wrong commodity and the wrong time.

He pursued his goals ambitiously and ruthlessly. He stopped slaughtering his cows for meat, and stopped milking them for dairy products. Instead he fed them night and day with tons of grass and collected all the manure in a large warehouse that had been used to house his wife's chickens. He filled it to the brim with dung and when he had enough he announced that he would no longer be paying taxes in rice and that all his financial transactions would be settled in dung.

'Please Samuel' his wife pleaded, 'don't do this to us.'

'You will see my dear' he said, 'soon everyone will see things my way. Dung is far superior as a form of money.'

He started taking the dung with him to town and insisting that people accept it as payment. But no one would touch it, and soon he got the nickname Stinky Stainbourn. His wife would scream at him. They were running out of food. Could he not just slaughter his cows for meat?

'No' he insisted. 'The dung standard will survive!'

But he was wrong. Two weeks later when the RGs came around to collect taxes and he tried to pay with dung, they arrested him and hanged him in the town square. They did not bother to confiscate the dung. Unfortunately his wife and young son were forced to move off the farm as all the cows began to die from ruptured stomachs, the result of over eating. The wife lived out the rest of her life in poverty, but the young boy grew up swearing not to be like his father.

—◦ V ◦—

A CHANGE OF MONEY

In which it is learned that slogans on coins are better when written in a foreign language.

The valley has now taken on the formal title The Valley, and those who live in it are called Valleyians. After two generations it seems that the public benefits brought about by taxation – working roads, public safety and so on – help increase prosperity to the point that the average Valleyian is still better off financially even after paying it. And it's during these years of increased stability and prosperity that the Valleyians start venturing further afield and interacting with other civilizations. Some traders make it their special business to import never before seen goods into the Valley, whilst others focus on providing foreigners with luxuries they lack. Some of course do both.

It's during the reign of Rich the Third that two things of great importance come into the Valley: the first is irrigation technology; the second is a yellow metal.

The irrigation technology is brought back by Julian Stainbourn aka Stainbourn II. Growing up with stories of his father's ruinous plans, he is highly conscious of the fact that a new form of money cannot be forced onto a population against its will. Money comes about naturally, and

20

the thing most suited to the purpose will ultimately win out. Until now rice farming has been limited to one area of fertile land controlled by Rich and a few other select farmers. Because rice cannot be grown without water, there has never been any threat of a newcomer entering the trade. But Stainbourn II is traveling in a nearby area when he meets some farmers that have mastered irrigation technology. He buys it off them and sets up a rice farm at the back of his house. He is fanatical about guarding the secret and slowly builds up his rice supply bit by bit. The RGs are not suspicious and for years he gets away with growing his own money. But then his teenage son, Sam Stainbourn aka Stainbourn III invites a friend around to play and shows him his father's setup. A few days later the friend's father rocks up and threatens to expose Stainbourn II if he doesn't show him how the technology works. Fearing for his family's safety he explains everything. The man has loose lips. The technology spreads at a rapid pace and everyone wants to get their hands on it.

Rich knows nothing about this new irrigation technology and doesn't realize for some time that anything is amiss. He keeps receiving taxes – in fact his rice vaults are virtually overflowing. But one day he decides to take a trip down to the market and notices a trader haggling with an old woman. The trader is shouting at her and demanding sacks of rice. The old lady insists she doesn't have any more. Rich asks the trader, 'why are you being so cruel to this old woman? She means no harm.'

The trader holds up some rice and says, 'this stuff isn't what it used to be.'

Rich is at first confused, but after taking a ride through the Valley on his trusted horse Boris, he notices that everyone has become a rice farmer. With this new imported technology, it seems, numerous farmers who had been involved in farming of other kinds, or different trades entirely, have converted their land into rice farms. The motivation was obvious: they all thought they could grow money. But the farm that had been in Rich's family since the time of Uncle Rice, was not the exclusive operation it had once been. Anyone could get water from the river to his land, and everyone was.

He retreats to his palace in frustration.

Then the yellow stuff comes to town. And when it comes, it keeps on coming. Suddenly it's everywhere and a tax collector explains that the citizens are no longer holding rice in the same quantities as they did in the past. The collector is not entirely certain as to what's going on, but thinks, that of their own volition, the citizens have started using this new substance as a store of wealth and a trading tool. Rich had foreseen that rice was no longer going to be the treasured store of wealth it had been in the past, but how the Valley would transition he'd had no idea. He summons the most affluent trader of the day and asks him to explain this phenomenon of the yellow metal more fully. The trader explains that there is a nearby valley equally blessed with resources and a wise government. However, instead of using rice as a store and measure of wealth, they use this yellow stuff called gold. As he, and many of the traders in the Valley, regularly do business with these foreigners, they've needed to acquire gold in order to pay for their goods. Some of the gold naturally made its way back into the Valley. The local Valleyians took a liking to it, and soon certain local traders began to accept it alongside rice. With the arrival of the irrigation systems and the sudden over-supply of rice, the appeal of gold has increased. It cannot be eaten, that much is true, but it can be used for decorative purposes, it's divisible, portable and fungible like rice, and it's far more durable, remaining in its current state for infinitely longer. The amount available in the earth is fixed. When a transaction takes place the quantity and quality of the gold is measured by the trader. He weighs it and hammers it out on a flat stone to test the purity: gold is peculiarly malleable. In the past, traders have struggled to carry large quantities of rice. What's more, the storerooms of some of the Valley's wealthy citizens are overrun with weevils, and with this sudden oversupply, it is losing its value by the day. And frankly, the citizens of the other valley see their rice-money as a form of peasantry. Gold fulfils its function as money better than rice does and is destined to take over. Mr. Rich cannot stop that. Gold is fairly difficult to extract and can only be enriched under certain conditions. The trader convinces Rich that if he is able to take control of the gold – and hence the money supply – his power will increase. If he fails to act now however, he will lose the power his family has held for generations.

Rich the Third is convinced. He enters into an agreement with the shrewd trader, whose job it is to locate and secure a source of gold. He locates a mine outside the valley borders and using borrowed technology, Rich and the trader open up a smelting operation. As the trader had predicted the change from one form of money to another was already underway and irreversible. But Rich is able to help facilitate a smooth transfer from one form of money to the next. He remains in control, and soon all taxes are levied in gold. This money indeed proves itself to be superior and the Valley's might continues to grow.

Unfortunately things did not go so well for the Stainbourn family. After the discovery of his irrigation system Stainbourn II became terribly ill and was soon bedridden. He had no idea what was going on in the outside world, knew nothing of the gold. His son, Stainbourn III took over the farm. When the 'new money' as he called it, came to the Valley he was highly skeptical. He would rant and sometimes hold sermons on his balcony, preaching to whomever would listen about the imminent decline of this stuff called gold. 'It will never last', he'd say.

'My family has studied monetary trends. And I can assure you that we are the experts! This yellow stuff is just a fad. It will pass, it will be gone soon!' he proclaimed.

He swapped not a grain of his rice.

This was a tumultuous time in the Valley and one evening a wealthy young man called Brian – 'Bright' Brian some called him – took a bet with Stainbourn III. He said, if rice remains the accepted form of money, I will give to you all my farms and my factory. If gold should take the place of rice, you must throw a feast and invite everyone in the Valley. You will boil your rice and together we'll eat it. Stainbourn accepted. Three years later, when it was officially announced that rice could not be used to settle payments or pay taxes, Stubborn Sam, as he became known, threw his party. The Valleyians ate rice for three days straight, until their bellies were bloated. The Stainbourn's were, once again, wiped out. Some say that this is where the phrase, 'putting your money where your mouth is' comes from.

Let us return to the tale of the new money. At first the government issues gold coins of a certain size and purity, but nobody trusts the coins and they always have to hammer them out to ensure that they are of their stated purity. The trader tells Rich that this is really slowing things down, but that there is a solution. He pulls out a coin from the neighboring valley – a people famous for their cheese making skills. On the coin is the face of one of their leaders and beneath it a slogan. In the language of the Cheesemakers it simply says, *Wir sind die Käser. Wir machen Käse.* Rich does not understand this language and is completely taken by it. The trader is happy and explains that as long as two governments recognize one another's power as legitimate, the face and emblem are understood as guarantees of the coin's purity. The coin and the country become bound in the mind of users, and so a debasement of the coin would be seen as a debasement of the organization that issues it.

'I will never debase!' cries Rich. 'This is just what we need!' he says, holding the gold coin up to the light. 'I love it! I love it!'

He comes up with an idea. In order to get the Valleyians fully behind the new currency, he will run a Valley-wide competition in which citizens must send in their ideas for the design of the coins. The citizen with the best design will win the first coin of the new batch to come off the mint. Rich puts up adverts for the competition across the Valley.

Suggestions pour in. The Fishers send in an image of a fish over flames, with the word *It Tastes Good* beneath it. The Baskets send in a picture of a fish caught in a trap with the words *We taught this to the Fishers*. Stainbourn III suggests having no image and the words: *This won't last long. You'll all sea.* (sic). Rich considers executing him for this, but his advisors inform him that they've already fulfilled their execution quotas for the month and that if they overdo it, the rope might begin to fray. Rich agrees that Stainbourn isn't worth it.

In another part of the Valley lives a group of people who consider themselves to be 'culturally distinct'. They refer to themselves as the Ventaks. Rich has never heard of them, but they don't like him at all. One night a farmer, Alfred Vonstoffle, takes out a piece of paper and draws a picture of Rich's face on it. Beneath it he writes the words *Rex Rich Tortoreous*, which in Ventak means, King Rich the Torturer. His wife whose sense of humor is as dark as his own laughs with him. Their eight year old boy however does not understand that to Rich himself this would be no laughing matter. He is proud of his father and the next day when his dad is off at work the little boy takes the suggestion and places it in the official entry box.

A week later at dinner time the door flies open and two RGs are standing there.

'Come with us!' they say, and take him by the arm. He'd noticed that the drawing had gone missing, and realizes at once what must have happened.

'It was just a joke!' Vonstoffle screams as they march him through the streets. 'No one was ever meant to see it!'

But the RGs are not interested.

In the pale moonlight Vonstoffle catches a glimpse of the gallows as they march him over the drawbridge towards Rich's castle. They pull a black sack over his head and Vonstoffle's knees go weak as he wets his pants. They seem to march him on forever and he becomes completely disorientated. He gets marched up a set of wooden stairs and hears the crowd chanting below. He wonders for a moment how they got there so quickly. But these thoughts vanish as he feels the rope coming around his neck. He whimpers gently, 'please, please forgive.'

'For what?' the voice of Rich booms, as he pulls the sack off Vonstoffle's head. 'You've won!' he says and smiles a smile so wide his face looks as if it might split.

Vonstoffle looks down to see that what he thought was a noose is in fact the ribbon to which his first edition gold coin has been tied.

'Thank you! Thank you all!' he says, and the crowd cheers.

He is surprised, to say the least. For of course he did not know that Rich, like so many leaders, has a fetish for coins minted with slogans in languages he cannot understand.

—∘ VI ∘—

BANKS

In which it is ascertained that no one needs all their money all the time.

Look at how the Valley has grown since its earliest days! The Valleyians' standard of living has continued to increase. The new money has improved the efficacy of trade. Fortunes have been made and lost. Love has come and gone, seasons turn to years and babies to adults. But still some waste their lives in frustration, unable to bring their dreams to fruition. Not because they lack vision or drive, but because they lack funding. Then one day a man called Milligan Banksy comes up with an ingenious plan. He will start the Valley's first bank, and name it in honor of himself. He'll call it a Bank, because the 'sy' part of his name sounds silly, and got him bullied at school. In fact he'll call it, Milligan's Bank.

He can barely contain his excitement. His plan, he believes, is truly revolutionary, and this is how it goes. For years, you see, Milligan has been a goldsmith. By his own admission he's not a particularly good one, and specializes in making flat plates because other things are a bit too complicated. He makes most of his income from charging clients a small fee to store their gold in a safe. Not a particularly interesting task either. A customer hands over a bag of coins and Banksy locks it up. If they want it back, he gives it to them. But he's always felt that he's never reached his true potential. After all he only became a goldsmith to satisfy his old man who's now long dead. But Banksy's brain has been ticking. He's noticed two groups in society. The first group is made up of people with ability but no money, the other of people with money but no ability. The latter, of course, constitute the majority of Banksy's customers. Furthermore he knows from decades of experience that very rarely does anyone come and ask for all their gold coins at the same time. In fact he can only think of one time in his whole career when this happened: the day Frank Knuckles – an RG – was caught sleeping with his boss's wife and had to leave town in a hurry. But never, not once, has every single one of his customers come and asked for all their gold on the same day. It's unthinkable. And what about all those young people who would give anything to get their hands on a bit of gold? If they had access to some money, surely they could find a better use for it. Money wants to be free. Is it not immoral to keep it away from those who could put it to good use? Is it not his duty, his destiny to facilitate this transaction? Yes, he concludes, it is!

Banksy decides that he will never lend out more than 30 percent of all the coins he holds. For coming up with this plan, and taking on the risk, Banksy will charge the most suitable borrowers a small fee, and this fee will be his reward.

The next morning on the busy main street the Valleyians see a new sign up on a previously vacant wooden building: *Milligan's Bank. Need money? Step inside.*

Not two hours pass before his first customer arrives. It's Johnny Robber, a good for nothing drunk who spends all his dad's money on booze and ladies.

'What do you need the money for Mr. Robber?' Banksy asks.

'Stuff', says young Johnny. 'You know, general stuff.'

Banksy climbs up from behind his desk and drags Johnny Robber onto the street by the scruff of his neck.

'Don't come back!' he yells, as he kicks him in the bum.

Half an hour later another young man arrives. His name is Sebastian Basket and he has an idea. He lays out a set of plans in front of Banksy. He has come up with a revolutionary new way to build ships. With these vessels the Valleyians will be able to take to the seas for the first time in history. They'll be able to see what lies beyond the horizon and find new trading partners. Banksy knows Sebastian's family, the Baskets. Not the wealthiest in the Valley, but decent, honest people. And Sebastian looks good for it. He explains the deal. He will lend young Basket the 100 gold pieces he needs to finance this operation. He will have to return the money by the end of the year, and pay an additional ten percent. In total, he will have to pay back 110 gold pieces. Sebastian is satisfied with the terms of this contract. They sign an agreement and Sebastian's life as a revolutionary ship-builder begins.

Banksy is soon able to lend out thirty percent of the coins, the limit he set himself, and while the money is out in the world, Banksy is a nervous man. He can be seen pacing at night, biting his fingernails and plucking out long strands of hair. But after the first year is up and the contracts come due, sure enough the money comes back and then some. He has made a ten percent profit on his investment and for a few days Banksy is as happy as he can ever remember being.

But then he starts to panic again. His stomach aches and contracts, he wheezes at night and sweats heavily from his forehead. For Banksy, you see, is a deeply superstitious man.

In his rooms at work hang stars and crosses and moons, rabbits' feet, foxes' tails and ducks' beaks. And they begin to talk to him and tell him that he's done wrong.

'That money wasn't yours' they seem to say. 'Other people gave it to you to look after, and you lent it out you slimy toad!'

He's thinking in particular about one of his longest standing customers, Mrs. Bread, in her fifties. Her husband recently died. She's getting old now and her knees and eyes aren't what they once were. In her younger days Mrs. Bread was a master craftswoman and her husband a well-loved baker. In their time together they managed to accumulate a fairly significant amount of wealth, and on her husband's death she was not left destitute. Banksy of course knows, as he currently holds just over a thousand gold coins of hers in his safe. She is still in generally good health and could live for years or decades, and though it's a substantial amount of money it will surely run out before then. And what will she do then? Beg? Steal? Starve?

No, Banksy decides, she will not!

He goes around to her house and knocks on her door. The gentlewoman lets him inside and says, 'hello Mr. Banksy. How are you today sir?'

'Mrs. Bread' he says, 'please forgive me.'

With that he places five gold coins on her table and says, 'these are yours.'

He explains what he's done and lays out his plan. He will always keep the majority of the money in the place that he now calls a bank. 'In honor of myself, you see.'

'Why don't you simply call it a banksy?' she asks.

'Because the sy part is silly!' he snaps, then apologizes for upsetting her.

She is very understanding and thanks him for his honesty. He explains that she will be able to draw a small yearly allowance without affecting her principal investment. If she needs to take out a large sum of money, that's fine, but correspondingly the amount of 'interest' that he will be able to offer her will decrease. She is more than happy to cooperate.

From there he travels to the homes of his various customers and tells everyone exactly what he's got up his sleeve. Many of his clients think it's a great idea. Some are not so happy about it, and he promises to keep their money in a separate vault.

Word gets out that the money Banksy was lending out wasn't his own, and that if you give your money to him, you too can get what some Valleyians are calling a 'magic salary'. Coins pour into Banksy's vaults and borrowers queue around the block for loans. His skill lies in determining the difference between a Sebastian Basket and a Johnny Robber. For this, he takes himself a cool five percent. He gives the other five percent to Mrs. Bread and his other customers. After all, with the massive increase in business, five percent comes to a lot. If he does this job properly – and he does – he facilitates the development of Valley industry, gives opportunity to those with ideas but no finance, and offers a salary to those who have worked all their life, but are now no longer able to do so. As his business grows he attracts a wide variety of clients. There are those who want to invest money with him, but do not need to draw any out each year. They simply want to know that their original investment is growing. On the other side there are those who want to borrow, but are unable to pay the principal amount all back in one year. He draws up different agreements depending on who is investing their money and who is borrowing it. His work becomes more complex but his function remains the same: facilitating the movement of money from those who have excess, but lack time, ability or ideas, to those who have none, but have an excess of ideas, ability and time.

Milligan Banksy is our Valley's first banker, and with his arrival two new concepts enter our Valley: credit and debt. Those who hand their money over to Milligan are creditors; those who accept it are debtors.

Milligan is the happiest he's ever been. He always knew that he was born for big things.

In these earliest days of banking, his institution does not increase the amount of money in circulation. He does not have the capacity to issue new money, yet he knows that by promising someone interest on their deposit, ten gold pieces have to become eleven; one hundred, one hundred and ten. These gold pieces, he knows, are themselves merely representations of true wealth that has been created somewhere in the world. So where does this extra wealth come from? Banksy is something of a philosopher and he spends many an evening alone on his porch drinking fine wines and smoking a large pipe. Interest, he concludes is added value: and value is measured in terms of a thing's usefulness to human beings. Added value is brought about through human skill, time, knowledge or labor. Ultimately it is always the process of taking something from nature and manipulating and changing it until it serves human needs more completely. A man takes a seed, plants it in the ground, it grows into a tree, he fells it, turns it into a ship that can sail the seas: it's usefulness to man has increased exponentially and accordingly the boat can be exchanged for more gold pieces than can the seed. It's nothing but chemistry and physics: man and nature: the gold itself, extracted from the earth, a unit of accounting, a way of measuring, promoting, expanding, but also constraining man's ability to manipulate his environment to satisfy his needs. Money is nothing. Logically it seems that any and all of these tasks can be performed without it. And yet, somehow he knows that they can't. He comes to conclude that having a unit of account, a way of measuring our progress in our conquest over our environment, is part of our own nature: much like our need to name the offspring we are driven to procreate. This system, he concludes, will always be central to human society and so must be carefully monitored and well maintained.

Banksy's son, Banksy II, does an apprenticeship under his father and when he's in his mid twenties goes into business himself. He also calls his business a bank, but plans to do things a little differently.

For years now our Valley's traders have been doing business with the Cheesemakers, and many are uncomfortable with carrying large quantities of gold on these sometimes treacherous journeys. Banksy II, in cooperation with some Cheesemaker businessmen, sets up another branch of his bank. Now, customers can deposit their money in the bank and be given a special receipt with Banksy's seal on it. This receipt can then be traded back for gold when the traveler arrives at his destination. For performing this service Banksy charges the customer a small fee. It is a very valuable service and yet it also creates a strange mutation in the nature of money. When the documents become more widely accepted, they are themselves sometimes used as tools of transaction. As such, while they are out in the world, acting as money, this money supply has effectively doubled: both the gold and the note can be used in an exchange transaction to acquire equal quantities of goods.

But Banksy II doesn't stop here. Whilst working under his father, he always thought that the old man was too conservative. Why does he keep seventy percent of the gold lying around in a safe when it could be out in the world earning interest? It's ridiculous! He's kept count and concludes that even keeping thirty percent of his money on hand is conservative. And so he starts lending big time. But the thirty percent that he leaves behind bugs him. Couldn't he lend out just a little bit more? Imagine how much interest he'd earn. So he lends out eighty percent, then ninety percent, then ninety five percent. And then something incredible starts to happen. The money that he's lent out is used by the borrowers to settle payments and purchase goods. The receivers of this money also come and deposit their money in young Banksy's bank. He lends it out again and again and again, and makes vast quantities of money. He hires workers to run his bank for him. He lives large, buys several carriages and numerous houses. He imports fine wines and cigars. He organizes himself countless concubines whom he puts up in a large mansion. When his father notices how much money his son is making, he asks him to explain exactly what he's doing.

'You're too old to understand dad' he says, but then sets out to explain it to him anyway.

'I understand very well, young fool!' says Banksy Snr. 'You have lent the same money out again and again to different people. Don't you think I've thought about this before? Didn't I teach you anything? Let me explain this to you. You took a hundred coins from customer A and lent them to customer B. Customer A has a claim on those coins. Customer B used the coins he borrowed from you and paid Customer C, who then chose to deposit them in your bank. He has an equal claim on those same coins! But you lent them all to customer D, who gave them to E, who deposited them with you and now also has a claim on them! Do you know what you're doing here? Do you?'

'Don't be so uptight dad' is all the young man can say. 'They won't all come at the same time.'

But the Valleyians have been keeping an eye on young Banksy, and word has gotten out that he's taking everyone for a ride. One day a messenger arrives at his mansion on the coast and explains that there are hundreds of people at his bank and they all want their gold coins.

'But I don't have them' he says.

'Please come and explain that to the mob, sir' says the messenger.

Banksy rides into town and sneaks in through the back of his bank. His employees are hiding in a back room. He walks past them and opens up.

'Morning everyone' he says, 'what a nice day it is.'

He hands over all the gold coins he has, hoping somehow that his confidence may calm the crowd and send the rest home.

But it doesn't, and when he runs out of coins he goes into the back room and yanks out his gold teeth. He rinses them off then puts them down on the counter in front of a customer.

'Those aren't gold coins!' the man says.

'Yes, they are. They just look different in this light. Now move along!' he says.

The crowd continues to swell and Banksy goes into his safe and takes out his gun. He goes into the room where his employees are hiding. He hands them some pliers and says, 'yank 'em out! Only the gold ones!'

All told he collects twenty teeth. But this isn't anywhere near enough to keep the ever swelling mob at bay. He sneaks out the back with his gun tucked inside his coat. He climbs into his carriage and is on route to rob his father's bank when the mob catches him and sets his carriage on fire. He runs for his life and dives into the nearby river. No one ever sees Banksy II again. He leaves behind a hugely disappointed father and freshly impregnated concubine.

—∽ VII ∾—
SHARES

In which it is learned that the pub can be more useful than the bank.

Sebastian Basket, Mr. Banksy's first borrower has done well. With his loan he secured himself timber, cotton and labor, and built the Valley's first ever ocean going vessel. He recruited as his captain a reformed convict called Mad Mike, and together, along with their fifteen crew members, the two men sailed for several months until they found an island, small in size, but rich in resources. At first they struggled to communicate, but soon each learnt the other's ways, and they developed a prosperous trading partnership. In particular the island people made large stone vases of extraordinary beauty that fetched high prices back in the Valley. They cultivated tasty spices, and made elegant jewelry. With the money he makes as the owner of the ship Mr. Basket is able to pay back his loan in less than a year. He is able to pay his men's salaries, much of which is spent on rum. But his ambitions have not yet been fulfilled, and the idea of a second ship starts sailing through his head. Though he has no doubt that he'll be able to pay back a second loan he is hesitant to get himself into debt again so quickly. Although not a superstitious man, he also wonders if he would always be

38

blessed with the same good fortune. He's seen the wild seas with his own eyes, and knows that a chance squall could sink a ship and all its loot. If he were lucky enough to float ashore, he'd avoid death but not debt. Making good on his loans without a means of earning is not something that appeals to him.

One night, sitting at the Valley's most popular upper-class drinking spot – The Rum and Drum – he gets talking to a man he's known since childhood. The fellow is none other than Theodore Fisher III, the eldest son of the current family head Theodore II. He is soon to come into a fortune, and already has a fair sum of money under his control. His family – having learnt early on the dangers of not diversifying – are looking to branch into new businesses, and so Theo – as his friends call him – makes an offer to Sebastian.

The offer goes thusly. He will put up however much money Basket needs to build a second ship. He will put up the capital to pay the new sailors' wages, and ensure that the boat is adequately stocked with rum and guns. In exchange he will own fifty percent of Basket's business. Should the trade route grow and prosper they will share evenly in the spoils, and side by side sip on expensive cognac. Should the ship sink or be attacked by pirates, they will equally suffer the losses, and if their lives are spared, together drown their sorrows. Young Basket orders his fifth rum for the evening, drains it at a single go, slams down his glass and offering his old friend a hand says, you have yourself a deal Fisher.

Fortune has shone on the two young men, and their wealth has grown rapidly. They are the golden boys of their families and heroes of the Valley. They come back with stories of riches and wonders that leave the Valleyians' jaws on the floor. Young men are desperate to emulate them and queue up to sign onboard as sailors. Young women are known to make an extra effort if they think they might run into them. But Basket and Fisher remain aloof, preferring to spend their time on land in private consultation. What exactly are they discussing each night at that corner table in the Rum and Drum? Some say they've seen strange things on the high seas: ghosts, monsters, women that sing songs too beautiful to resist, or femme fatales with fish's tails. In truth they've seen something different entirely; something perfectly earthly but just as enticing.

On one of the voyages, they docked their ship at night just a few miles short of the island, and noticed something they'd never seen before. It must have been because the night was unusually clear and the sea strangely quiet. But out on the darkness, on the very edge of the world, they noticed a shimmering light. The next day they confirmed their suspicions. The island was not alone. It was part of a string, perhaps an entire chain: tens, hundreds, thousands? And what did they lead to? Another land mass? A new continent? Could it really be? They sent a single crew member onto land, and he confirmed that the next island along was indeed inhabited. On the journey home, they noticed in the distance another ship, not their own. Its flag was crimson in colour and they understood that they were not alone in their lust for wealth.

They come to the conclusion that they have to act and act now. Two ships will not be enough, neither will three or five. They have to go all-out and dominate the route before someone else does. Neither have the capital, but buzzing with confidence they decide to approach the now graying, respectable old gentleman, Mr. Banksy of Milligan's Bank.

They offer their condolences for the untimely death of his son.

'I always told the young whipper snapper he could not rely on tier two capital' he says. 'Gold teeth for god's sake! Gold teeth!' He slams his hand on the desk.

When he's calmed down they thrash out their proposal, and ask if they can have funding for ten new ships. He says he can see the gleam in the boys' eyes, but it is just too much money and far too dangerous. He can sponsor a single ship, but an entire fleet would require half the money in his vaults. And this is not money that can be lost: families entrust him with their livelihoods and how can he gamble it all on a single adventure? What if a squall wipes out their entire fleet? No, it is too risky, he simply can't do it.

The two leave disappointed, but not dejected. For a moment they wish Banksy II were still in business. But they soon turn their minds back to the present reality. They are nothing if not inventive. They concoct another plan, and immediately put it into effect.

Every Thursday evening at the Rum and Drum a group of ten of the Valley's richest men meet for a round of drinks and their chitchat usually revolves around money. Our two entrepreneurs are familiar with some of them, and their families are well known in the Valley. Come Thursday they buy the men a round of drinks and lay out their plan in detail. They need to raise enough money to build ten ships and pay for ten crews and they need to do it now. They want to offer these select gentlemen – who are shrewd and pride themselves on being ahead of the pack – a unique opportunity to each own one tenth of the business. The young men had calculated exactly what it would cost. The investors will be issued with a certificate that indicates this ownership. It entitles them to one tenth of the company's profits. But more than this, the certificate – which they call a share – will be a new form of asset: just like a physical commodity such as fish, gold or baskets. After they purchase it at its designated cost, Basket and Fisher will not be able to determine its resale value. The investors will be able to sell it to whomsoever they chose at whatever price they are able. The new owner will then acquire the rights to the stated share of the company's profits, and secure the right to sell it on at whatever time he chooses, at whatever price he's able. How much someone is willing to pay for the share will be determined, presumably, by how profitable the company is, what its future prospects are and what state its fleet and crew are in. Should they discover that the string of islands bears treasures beyond even their wildest imaginations, should their ships sail strong and their crews remain loyal, the value of the shares could double, triple, or even grow a hundred fold. On the other hand, should all ten ships be wiped out in a squall on their maiden voyage, the shares will be worth their weight in household fuel.

It is a massive risk, but apparently one worth taking, as all ten men reach for their money sacks and exchange their gold for paper. These men are our Valley's first shareholders.

—ᴄ VIII ᴄ—

BONDS

In which the government learns the art of borrowing.

Basket and Fisher's Oceanic Enterprises, as their company is known, has become extraordinarily successful, and the shareholders have grown obscenely wealthy. Most of them can no longer fit into their old suits, but this hardly matters. They buy new ones. Basket and Fisher themselves, have grown into cult like figures in the Valley. They no longer sail onboard their own ships, and mostly direct operations from their headquarters on land. The Valley has been fortunate and avoided any major crisis. All have prospered together, and each innovation has brought about an increase in the general good. Contact with outsiders likewise has been mutually beneficial. But then one day, Mad Mike, the trusty captain of Basket's first, and still flagship, Basket One, comes crashing into the Rum and Drum with awful news.

'Those Island maniacs are coming! They want to kill us all!' screams the crazy redheaded, red-faced beast of a man.

The truth of the matter is that the Valleyians had been trading with the Island people for some time without any major conflicts arising. But recently, the demand for a certain oil extractable only from trees that grow on islands a few miles off the east coast of the Island has dramatically increased. The price of oil has gone up and some Valleyian traders have started cutting down the trees without the Islanders' permission. They claim that these freestanding islands are not the property of the Island. In response to this the Island set up a garrison on the largest of these small islands – Palmus Major – and tensions have continued to rise. One night Mad Mike led his drunken, well armed men in attack against the lightly armed garrison. The attack turned into a bloody massacre from which only a few managed to survive. They returned to the Island and the story spread. The Islanders are now angry and are on their way to take revenge.

An official investigation is opened into Mad Mike's conduct. On the inquest form under the heading – Reason for Committing Massacre – he writes, *'I was over-armed, over-boozed, and under-intelligenced.'* The government could find no grounds on which to disagree with him.

More importantly however, the government needs to prepare for the attack and Regina Rich, aka Rich IV instructs her top generals to prepare for battle. That night the army wages its first war, and is able to defend the Valley until sunrise when the enemy ships retreat. Lives have been lost, but the Valley has been spared. For now. The queen and army are convinced that the enemy will attack again and this time it will be more serious. Their only chance for survival is to follow them into the seas and thrash them.

Unfortunately the enemy are just as hardy and shrewd as the Valleyians and victory does not come swiftly. This places the leadership, army, citizens, and industry of the Valley in a situation they have never before found themselves. They must build ships and armory, recruit young men into the army, pay their salaries and fill their stomachs. They are forced overnight to redirect their entire economy and the duty to lead this operation and more specifically to finance it, falls on Rich IV and her government.

The war puts enormous strain on government finances. In fact, after just several months, Rich IV is facing a situation that would have seemed unthinkable in any previous generation: she and her government are almost bankrupt. They have used up all their tax revenue, and if they are unable to keep up their financial commitments the war machine will grind to a halt and the Valley will be overrun by the enemy. It is simply unthinkable.

Regina invites the aging Banksy and some of the Valley's wealthiest men, including the now middle-aged Basket and Fisher, to her palace. She lays it on the line for them: without funding we're all going to die. Now come up with a plan.

Before the night is over they have hatched a new scheme. In fact it is so obvious, they wonder why they haven't been doing it all along. In the past, citizens with excess wealth have placed it into Milligan's Bank and received a modest interest. The wealthier citizens have had the option of investing in businesses such as Fisher and Basket's. But now there will be a new form of investment, and any one who loves the Valley will see that it is the investment of choice. They will issue something called bonds, and they will work in a similar way to the shares issued by Fisher and Basket. The buyers will not own a stake of the government as such, but they will be entitled to the repayment of the loan in full with interest, and the interest rate will be higher than that they could achieve by leaving their money in the bank. The decision to invest in bonds is also rational for the reason that, should they win the war they will have complete control of the disputed trading area and numerous resources including the much sought after palm oil. This will bring prosperity to the Valley increasing the government's tax revenue. Although they will not use this as part of the marketing scheme, it should be understood by would-be investors that their money is safer with the government than with anyone else: because they have the right to tax, and more than this, they have control of the mint. Whilst promoting these bonds, they will be able to draw on public sentiment and play to emotion. It's our Valley! We're all in this together!

Banksy allows them to use the empty building behind his bank as a market to sell these bonds. A sign that reads simply, Bond Market, goes up on the front of the building and halfway through the first day they've sold numerous bonds and are confident that their plan is a winner.

Word spreads and soon the Valleyians are clambering to get their hands on a bond. At first they offer a six percent yield – the buyer will get his money back, plus six percent in interest. After one year, the army has managed to secure certain palm tree growing islands, and are selling the oil for large profits. Regina levies an especially high tax on oil sales. With this increased revenue the government is able to pay back these bonds in full with the six percent interest they promised. It's now clear to the public that this investment is as good as putting your money in the bank, and so accordingly, the government is able to lower the yield, and now only offers five percent on top of the original investment.

The war rages on for years and soon the government once again finds itself in dire straits. It is forced, much against its will, to visit the Cheesemakers and try to entice them with their government bonds. Some of the financial types – those who like to sip brandy and smoke cigars and talk about financial things – refer to these bonds as, 'external debt'. Some whisper that this borrowing may be riskier than internal borrowing, because the foreigners don't care much for Regina and her people, and should things go wrong they won't be able to appeal to their sense of patriotism.

The neighboring Cheesemakers send a delegation to our Valley. The head financier, a thin man with oily hair and a pencil-like moustache, explains that if he is to make, what would amount to a fairly significant investment in the Valley's government, he needs to do a thorough investigation. He looks at the government's books, inspects the state of the industry and does his best to gauge the morale of the people. He is satisfied that, despite the ongoing war, the Valley is in order – the financial institutions appear sound and the people and government honest and hardworking. But he is concerned about the large amounts of money that the Valley has already had to borrow. They are deeply in debt and this is business, not charity. He'll be at the bond market early tomorrow morning, but he can't promise that he's going to buy up bonds at the current going rate of five percent.

The next morning the bond market is, as always, a hive of activity. But today is an historical day: the first time a foreign buyer will be present in the hallowed halls. The government has developed a set way of issuing new bonds. In the interest of securing the lowest possible interest rate for itself, it holds an auction. It offers them at the lowest rate of the day, and if it has buyers, it sets that as the current bond yield. But today no one seems to be buying. They understand that the government has to raise massive amounts of capital – more than it has ever needed to do in the past – and the citizens are anxious to see what the foreigner will accept. After all, it could be that he knows something they do not. After much tension and sweating, the foreigner finally offers to buy the vast quantities of government debt at a rate of eight percent, three percent higher than in the past. The government has no choice but to accept. Citizens and private traders begin to worry that their money is no longer safe with their own government and so in order to compensate for their taking on the increased risk, they too demand what the foreigner demanded.

This is very bad for our government. The price of borrowing money has now gone up significantly and this means that each year a substantially larger portion of their budget will be spent in simply paying back the interest on their loans. This will drive them further into debt, and force them to borrow more money. When investors see how much they are borrowing, they will begin to doubt their ability to pay the loans back at all, and as a reward for taking on the ever-growing risk they will demand ever-higher returns. This will mean setting aside even more money to pay back the interest on loans, which will necessitate even more borrowing. And so the death spiral will begin.

Our government it seems is doomed.

But then, the gods must have chosen to smile on them, for they strike gold. Literally.

—❦ IX ❦—

INFLATION

In which our Valley strikes the root of wealth, learns the art of alloying, and causes both happiness and misery.

It happens one evening when our queen, Regina, aka Rich IV, is on the verge of a nervous breakdown. The head miner arrives at her quarters and explains that they have struck a vein of gold deeper and richer than anything they have ever seen in their many years of mining. The queen commandeers a wagon and rides out to the mine to see it for herself. On inspection, she is convinced. She is blessed, she believes, and the Valley will surely prevail.

She commands the miners to work around the clock in shifts, and starts conscripting young men from the Valley to work as miners. She instructs her army to bring any enemy captives back to the Valley and chain them up, pick in hand. The mine runs twenty four hours a day seven days a week and the ore is taken to the refinery and the metal to the mint. The mint, like the mine, runs all day without cease and before long Regina's vaults are overflowing with gold coins. She laughs so hard that her sides ache. She drinks the most expensive champagne, and eats food that she doesn't even like, provided it's expensive.

She instructs her men down at the market to stop selling bonds: she has her own money now! She pays the salaries of the soldiers herself, finances all the industry through her freshly minted gold coins, and gives her officers and best performing soldiers significant bonuses. With this new and infinite supply of money she decides that she will drive the war effort harder than ever and doubles her orders for ships, guns and explosives. The captains of industry start living it up and the men down at the mills are given healthy bonuses as the owners compete to keep them on.

Soon there are unprecedented amounts of gold coins in circulation, and this starts to have a number of unintended consequences. The boat makers tell Regina that the price of boats is going up. When she asks why, the boat maker explains that the price of wood has increased. Regina sends her men to the timber lands to find out why these stingy bastards are screwing her over by charging more for wood. They have no choice, they say. The lumberjacks are demanding more money because everything they buy has become more expensive. Oh well, she doesn't care she says. If prices have gone up then they've gone up! She'll conscript even more miners to mine more gold and open up a second mint. That way she can keep up pace with these price increases.

The plan seems to work, and as prices go up, she mints more coins. But because prices are constantly on the rise producers at various points on the production line are anticipating price increases before they take place and compensating for them. In other words, a man whose business it is to import wood from an outlying region of the Valley and sell it to the sawmills, knows that by the time he gets back to the timber lands the price of wood is going to have gone up. Therefore he demands higher payment from the man at the sawmill in order to ensure that he isn't out of pocket. The man at the sawmill in turn charges the boat maker more. This process continues with each round of production, and each rise in prices necessitates more minting of money, until eventually there is not enough gold in the ground for Regina to keep up.

She is again on the verge of mental collapse when one of her mint workers – a hunchback named Terrence Tamper, who speaks with a lisp – suggests making some minor alterations to the coins' constituent elements. At first the idea shocks Regina.

'That is my grandfather's face on that coin, Tamper, you slithering bastard! Have you no shame?'

But Tamper explains that it is the face itself – and everything it stands for: the power and reliability of Regina's government – not the metal that gives the coin its value. These words fan Regina's vanity like wind over flames, and she asks Tamper to continue as she lights up her slim white pipe.

Traders have long since ceased hammering the coins flat to test them, says the hunchback, and he knows how to mix copper with gold in just the right quantity to make the coins indistinguishable from pure gold ones. He has a cousin who runs a copper mine and he swears that if they give him a few bars of pure gold they can secure several tons of copper.

'Tons?' Regina asks, her face turning purple.

'Yeth', says Tamper, 'tonths'

Regina tells him to get to work and a week later Tamper brings her two coins: one pure gold, one a mixture of gold and copper. He asks Regina to tell him which is which. Regina holds them up to the light, looks at them from different angles, and admits that they are indistinguishable. Tamper tells her that with this new scheme in place they can

51

increase their coinage three fold. Regina laughs so hard she almost dies. She opens up two new mints and employs a hundred new smelters – all are sworn to secrecy on pain of death.

The monetary boom gives the war effort that final boost it needs, and the Valleyians are literally weeks away from wrapping up the campaign, when one of the weapons builders refuses to accept payment in Regina's coins. Regina is furious. The manufacturer explains that none of his suppliers are accepting *Rex Rich Toterous* coins. Each week there are more and more coins in the Valley and so no one is able to effectively price their own goods. More and more Valleyians it seems are point blank refusing to accept the coins as tender – and although the trader does not have the nerve to say it outright, he hints at the fact that the coins may no longer be made from pure gold.

In her fury Regina rips the trader's leather purse off his belt and pours the coins onto the floor. She bends down and picks one up, and holding it to the light sees a palm tree and the words *We Islanders Stand As One*. She realizes that, having lost faith in her money, her own citizens are using another region's coins within her own borders. She is furious!

Regina chases the trader with a big stick and threatens to, 'boil his children!'

To hell with these lazy, unappreciative Valleyians, Regina thinks. I was doing all this for their good anyway! Now she'll have to source whatever she needs from suppliers outside the Valley. They still respect the face of her grandfather.

For some time this works and she temporarily causes a boom in neighboring regions. She stimulates their various economies and encourages large-scale increases in the exports of commodities. Regina gets what she needs and the exporters in the neighboring regions grow wealthy. Or so they think. When the neighbors start demanding more 'gold' coins for their products, Regina gets Tamper's cousin to send them more tons of copper. She expands the smelters and mints again and employs yet more workers, and threatens to kill them if they breathe a word. If those other bastards want more coins, more coins they'll get. She's played this game before.

But soon Regina gets a visit from the Cheesemakers. The delegate is angry, and his face is red.

'We two have been doing business for generations' he says, 'and traders in each region have accepted coins from the other as legal tender. This has helped foster good trade relations. For this we were both grateful.'

But he has now witnessed a full-scale displacement in his region: the *Rex Rich Toterous* coins have come flooding in, and resources of all kinds have gone flowing out. They have millions of coins, but no wood, rice, wheat, cotton, or iron. The only logical thing for him to do – so he thought – was to melt them down and turn them into coins with his own government's signature on them. But when attempting to do this, he noticed that these so-called gold coins are in fact over sixty percent copper! Now, not only have all their resources been sucked out of their region, but those loans that Regina has been repaying are denominated in coins that have massively decreased in value. The citizens in his region have started hammering down the coins again to test them. They've lost faith in *Rex Rich Torterous* and would rather hold on to whatever little scraps of commodities and goods they have than trade them for worthless coins. When traders do accept coins, they demand massive quantities of them in expectation of the price increases that they predict will have occurred before they are able to pay for the goods they need to produce their own. The price of everything in his own region is going through the roof and he doesn't have access to a magic golden vein like Regina, nor is he so completely lacking in moral fiber as to mix his coins with crap. In short, this operation of Regina's has caused havoc.

The queen offers him a cup of tea and a kumquat and explains that the coins are pure gold and that if anything else has gotten into them, she has no idea how. The man asks if he can inspect her mints, but Regina fakes a seizure and has the delegate escorted back to his own region.

A few days later Banksy calls on her and explains that his bank is on the verge of going under. He had denominated all his loans in coins minted by Regina's government and with the massive increase in circulation, borrowers had access to vast quantities of coins. They have been able to pay their loans back over night, but the coins are now unable to buy anything near as much as they could in the past. The debtors are being let off the hook, and the savers are watching their investments turn to dust, because he is unable to offer them returns that keep pace with the rate of price increases. Our Valley – and the surrounding areas – are caught in the grips of serious inflation. We can only thank our lucky stars that at this point, the war draws to its conclusion. The enemy had completely run out of resources, but had they been able to fight for just another few months our government would have been completely unable to finance its war effort, and our Valley would have been decimated.

—◦ X ◦—

CENTRAL BANKS

In which it is learned that smoke and mirrors work magic in restoring confidence.

The war comes to an end but economic conditions deteriorate. There is serious and widespread poverty, and with Regina's coins accepted only in massive quantities and often not at all, the Valleyians have in many cases returned to barter. This of course is not sustainable and under the advice of the ancient Milligan Banksy, Regina removes all the coins that the Valleyians refer to as debased, from circulation. She melts them down, and separates the gold from the copper.

After publicly announcing that she knew nothing about Terrence Tamper's scheme – and having him beheaded in the town square – she gets to work on reissuing a new set of coins. Regina had grown up believing that coins would be respected if their inscriptions were in a foreign language. But after the recent inflation debacle she has come to doubt these assumptions. Instead she wants a coin minted in her own language. She wants no slogan, only an image of her own face and the words *Hon. Regina*: short for Honorable Regina.

She gives these instructions to Terrence Tamper's replacement, Calvin Coin. She explains to her government that she will be taking an extended vacation at her summer cottage, Bretton Estate, and that when she returns she expects the coins to be in circulation. All taxes from now on are to be levied in the new coins only, thus coercing the citizens into accepting them.

She enjoys her vacation and even finds the time to start penning her memoir, *A Queen's Life. The Inside Story.* But she returns to a nasty shock. On arriving at her castle she finds one of the new coins sitting on a counter. The queen on this coin has an enormous nose that extends halfway down to the words: *Hor. Regina.*

'Hor Regina!' she screams at the top of her voice.

Her lady in waiting comes running to her chambers and explains that the die had a flaw.

'Yes, I can see that!' she says. 'My nose looks like a cucumber! Haul these things out of circulation now!'

But the lady in waiting says that this is not possible, and beckons the top government officials to come help her explain.

'Unfortunately madam' her top aide says, 'we have already distributed them throughout the Valley, and used up all of our gold in making them.'

'How can this be?' she screams.

'And it gets worse madam. The citizens have interpreted the hor. To stand for horrible. And unfortunately madam some of the Valleyians are now referring to you as Regina the horrible.'

'This is unbearable' she says, collapsing on a chair. 'Well, at least it's only some of them that call me that.'

'The others madam, call you Regina of the long nose.'

She wails for a moment before instructing her top aide to bring her Calvin Coin and a blunt axe. She ties him up herself and cuts off his head.

She spends a few days in depression, sulking around her room and drinking bloody marys. But soon she regains her spirits. After all, she doesn't much like her own citizens so what difference does it make if they don't like her? They're all peasants anyway, and most of them don't bath. Perhaps Regina the horrible is not the worst name to be known by. She doesn't even need to pretend to be nice anymore and a big nose is a sign of strength. She flips the pure gold coin up and down a few times and decides that in fact she rather likes it. She sends out an official decree saying that from this time forward the new money will be known as Regina the horrible – RTH coins.

Soon a delegation from the neighboring Cheesemakers pays her a visit and asks that she repay her loans in the newly denominated – pure gold – RTH coins. She insists that those bonds were issued in the old currency and she considers them to have been settled in the old currency.

'Let bygones be bygones' she says. 'We all have things we're not a hundred percent happy with. And we've finally brought about stability, let's not get any funny ideas in our heads.'

Similarly, the citizens that bought her bonds during the war were repaid in worthless coins that were later taken out of circulation. She explains that this is an inevitable consequence of progress. After all, those pesky Islanders that started the war have been thrashed and there's really no point harking on about it.

The Valley has entered a state of relative depression, but the chaos of the war and the inflation seems to have subsided and Regina is confident that economic activity will pick up with time. Until then she has a large collection of cigarillos to smoke and some fine port extracted from the cellar of The Island people's leader. She is just lighting up on her balcony one evening when a messenger arrives bearing news.

Although Regina is hardly aware of their existence – and knows nothing about their involvement in the *Rex Rich Torterous* debacle – The Ventak People have grown in strength and number and cemented their place as 'cultural separatists' in the fertile northern regions of the Valley. They worship a deity named Mr. Tak, in whose honor they have built a large wooden statue, at the feet of which they burn one third of their yearly rice supply.

'Is this some kind of joke?' Regina asks the distraught looking messenger.

'No', he insists, 'this is no joke.'

But he has not come to discuss the merits of idol worship. What Regina needs to understand is that the leaders of the Ventak people have been in conversation with Mr. Tak and Mr. Tak does not like Regina. He finds her disrespectful and does not believe that his followers should live under her aegis.

'Get to the point!' Regina yells.

'The Ventak have declared themselves independent, elected their own leader, and put together a fairly sizeable army. They insist that your majesty officially recognize their independence and free them from your rules and tax regime.'

'I see' says Regina, pulling hard on an Island cigarillo.

'And more than this your majesty' the messenger continues, 'the area they want as their own is positioned right on top of the largest gold mine in the entire Valley.

'Impossible!' Regina yells. 'Then we must fight them!'

She summons her generals and tells them to prepare for war. They complain that the soldiers are war-weary and will not be willing to take up arms.

'Willing?' Regina yells. 'I'm not asking if they'd like to go to war, you morons! Line them up, guns in hand!'

The tired army is now forced to fight against the men they'd recently been fighting alongside. And the fighting is brutal. The Valley's army manages to contain the Ventak Separatists – as they've called themselves – within their own borders. But there's no sign that they'll surrender and very soon Regina is facing the same problem she so recently encountered. She has no money!

Since the time of the new currency the bond market has been closed, as Regina did not need to raise any finances. But after one month of war she orders the bond market reopened and places signs around the town advertising this lucrative and safe investment. At eight am the following morning when doors open there are two people standing outside. One is an elderly woman who misread the advertisement and thought they were giving away free cocoa. The other is a charlatan who'd hoped to use this auction as a means of singling out the biggest morons in the Valley.

But no one, not even the biggest moron, is stupid enough to fall for this scheme.

Not to worry, she'll call up her friends the Cheesemakers.

The envoy arrives at lunch the next day and Regina explains that she is willing to offer them a very lucrative deal: government bonds with an eight percent yield. When the envoy hears this he is in the process of nibbling on a cracker. He laughs so hard he chokes to death.

Regina believes that her hands are tied and she is in the process of sourcing new copper and hiring new minters, when Milligan Jnr, Banksy's second son, pays her a visit. His father died a few months before, and he has taken control of the bank. (No one ever talks about his brother anymore). He sits Regina down and explains that she is about to commit a terrible mistake. If she fires up the mint again and starts issuing millions of debased coins like she did last time, surely she knows what will happen. But this time, it will only happen quicker as her suppliers are already wise to her ways.

'But what am I meant to do then?' she asks. 'No one will lend me any honest money.'

'Your problem madam', he says, 'if I may be so bold as to say, is one of public relations. Everyone thinks you're a scoundrel, and after the way you acted last time I can't say I blame them.'

Regina begins to turn red, but Milligan Jnr. cools her temper by explaining that he has a solution: one that can work in everyone's favor.

'We just need a couple of mirrors and a good deal of smoke, and I can get you looking like the safest bet in town again. Here's your problem madam, it's hanging around your neck: that big silver key to the mint.'

'But this is my favorite' she says, stroking it. 'I even had a big plum colored jewel placed in the centre. Look!'

'I do not question your taste madam. We all agree that you have impeccable style. But so long as you have that particular key, not even the biggest fool will trust you. No one will lend you a cent when they know you can turn their investment into rubbish. So here's what you need to do. Give me the keys to the mint madam, and the right to issue currency. Allow me to be your banker, the man who runs your books. I have a significant amount of capital in the new currency in my vaults, and I know my wealthy clients will be happy to go along with this new idea. I will lend you all the money you need to get you through the next few months. Potential investors will see that it is in my best interest to get that money back from you, and to get it back in coins whose value has not been depreciated. It would be economic suicide for me to fire up the mint, debase the coins, and devalue my own investment. What's more, I will determine how much you are able to borrow, and because I always want to protect my own investments I won't let you go into debt you cannot repay. When everyone sees that you have been duly reigned in, they will be happy once again to lend to you. In exchange for this, as I have already said, I will lend you the money you need right now. More than that, I have noticed other banks starting up in this Valley. Now I don't mind a bit of competition, but when it comes to you and I madam, I will admit to being a little possessive. No other banks are allowed to lend to you directly! Only me! I am your banker! I run your books! Private citizens can buy your bonds and so can foreign powers. All through me of course. And as for other banks, well, I'll decide just how much and when. But I'm your banker, you see. Do we have ourselves a deal?'

Regina, realizing that she has no choice but to believe this crazy banker, shakes his hand, and the two proceed to the balcony. A key is handed over. A contract giving Milligan Jnr. and his bank a thirty year license as The Banker of the Valley is signed. And of course, cigarillos and cigars are smoked.

When word gets out that Regina and her government have been brought to heel, interest again emerges in the bond market. When she manages to repay her first set of loans without resorting to the mint, offers start coming in, and very soon she is able to secure funding for her war effort at interest rates even lower than those offered by Milligan's bank. With the massive inflow of capital she is able to crush the Ventak rebellion.

Milligan Jnr. suggests that she should not wipe out the Ventak people, as she seems so eager to do. Instead he suggests a meeting with their leaders in which they offer them a certain degree of independence. Allow them to have their own customs and their own religion. Let them wear what they like and talk whatever language they feel comfortable talking. They may even have their own laws and their own banks. But their currency must be the Valley's currency, and their taxes must be paid to the capital. Regina likes the idea, and from her position of strength is able to get the Ventaks to agree to these terms.

Even after the peace comes Milligan still has 28 years on his contract as the government's banker. He heads up what becomes known as the Central Bank, and he, not Regina keeps the key to the mint. He, not Regina, is in charge of monetary supply. He is our Valley's first ever central banker.

─ XI ─
STOCK MARKETS AND FUTURES CONTRACTS

In which it is learnt that you must be careful in selling something you don't have.

Following the Valley's conquest of the Ventak people – a victory that came about in large part thanks to Milligan Jnr's creative banking scheme and Regina's regained credibility – a new period of stability and prosperity arrives in the Valley. The Ventak are granted the cultural independence they desire and provided they pay their taxes on time are allowed to continue burning one third of their crop to please Mr. Tak. With time it is revealed that Mr. Tak is satisfied with a mere ten percent of their yield, and this leniency on the deity's part helps further boost their productivity and hence Regina's tax intake. The idea of cultural and religious independence but fiscal unity appeals to several smaller, previously independent states, and in the decades that follow a number of them accede to the Valley State. On accession they gain access to many of The Valley's advanced institutions and are entitled to military protection. Their economies also benefit from the relaxing of trade barriers. Regina eventually dies at the age of ninety three, her memoirs still incomplete. She is buried at Bretton Estate.

Her son Rich V takes over and his government continues to benefit from the constant broadening of their tax base. This also helps them pay off their loans to foreign lenders quickly, and further strengthens the image of the Central Bank as a stabilizing force. When the thirty year license expires, it is renewed and Banksy's son takes over as the new central banker.

It's during these years of prosperity that a grandson of one of the original investors in Basket and Fisher's Shipping Enterprise comes up with an enterprising idea. He has inherited his family shares and though they have increased enormously in value since their original purchase – in fact relative to any other investment over the same time period they've proven themselves to be the best – young David Buysell believes that the time to sell has come. The way he sees it, Basket and Fisher's will continue to grow for the foreseeable future, but they will never again grow at the rate they have done during their earlier years. They have reached a stable plateau, and that is good. But Buysell sees about him a new generation of entrepreneurs with gleaming eyes, and he wonders if he can identify the next Basket and Fisher. If he were able to do so, he could use the enormous profits his family has made in that legendary boating enterprise and buy up share positions of equal size in five or ten companies that are only starting up and hence valued at far less.

He believes also that normal men and women, not only the financial elite should be able to invest in new and exciting enterprises. Anyone with a supply of surplus wealth and a greater appetite for risk than bank savers and bond buyers should be able to buy and sell shares. Should his idea work, young entrepreneurs, or those looking to expand their businesses, will have a new means of raising capital without going into debt. Businesses will issue a certain number of shares at a certain price. Investors will buy them and thereafter be entitled to a percentage of the company's earnings, and have the right to sell the shares at whatever price they are able to get. He needs to create a market where these buy sell transactions can take place with ease. He looks to the bond market as a successful model, and so decides that on the same street, on the opposite side, he'll erect a brown wooden building with white terraces and a red roof. He hires a local artist to design a sign with the words, *Stock Exchange*, painted on it. He hangs it up and declares himself open for business.

The stock market proves to be another popular innovation. Fortunes are made and fortunes are lost and soon a new profession has arisen. Within months of the opening, a pair of shrewd brothers from the wealthy Lyst family, both named Alan, come up with a scheme. The two brothers split up. The elder Alan goes to the floor and finds out what companies are trading for and watches the movement of their stock on a daily basis. The younger Alan takes to the streets and does some investigation into these companies. He tries to gather what their future prospects are, determine if they've had to go into debt to get started, find out whom they are in competition with, and how good their managers and workers are. Based on this he'll do his calculations and work out what the company is worth. The two brothers then meet in their offices across the street from the stock market and compare notes. If they decide that a company is trading for less than what the younger Alan calculated its worth to be, they will put it on their buy list. The elder Alan will continue to watch the price movements and wait until it becomes available at their target price, and then make the purchase. If their calculations are correct, in time the company will start to do well. When it does, other investors will desire the shares more than they had in the past, and hence the value of the two Alans' shares will rise. When they're satisfied with the profit they've made they'll sell. They call this 'going long'. After doing this for several years, the brothers come across another idea. If they feel that a share is selling for more than its real value (compared to what their calculations valued the company at), they will pay the owner of the share a small fee to borrow it from him. Then they will sell it to someone else and set the money aside. When word gets out that the company is a dud, the share value will drop and they'll buy it back at a reduced price, and return it to its original owner. Their profit is made in subtracting the lending fee and the buy-back price from the original sell price. They call this 'going short'. And so, no matter what happens the Alan Lysts can make money.

Some think this scheme dishonorable, as the two men appear to be making lots of money without adding any value to the Valley's economy. But as their trading skills and confidence grows the two buy a larger office across the street from Milligan's bank and set up a business open to the public. Now, if you have money but lack confidence in your trading abilities you can give it to the Lysts and they will use their skills to invest it for you where and how they see fit. The increased interest in the stock market that their professional service creates naturally means that larger amounts of money come into the market. This creates something that the brothers refer to as liquidity. An increase in available money means that would-be investors can buy shares quickly and get rid of them quickly. It also means that newly listed companies with good prospects can quickly raise the money they need to finance their operations.

The street now home to Milligan's original bank, The Bond Market and the Stock Exchange, has become known as Banksy Street in honor of the Valley's first financial innovator. The Rum and Drum has turned into a franchise and has opened up a new branch on the street. It is a popular spot for traders, bankers and businessmen, and occasionally some Valleyians not involved in the financial industry will pop in for a drink. It's here one evening that we find Warren Stainbourn, the descendant of a dung standard enthusiast, an irrigation importer and a rice eater. The story of Stubborn Sam, the rice eater, is by far the most famous and has become a part of Valley lore. The Stainbourns have for generations had to bear the shame of this black mark against their name. No one in the family eats rice, not even with curry. And to this day heartless children and drunks will hiss 'rice-eater' under their breath when a Stainbourn walks down the street. But Warren has come far in turning the family's fortunes around. His father was a wheat farmer and as a child Warren lived comfortably. Unfortunately however one night, his father, for reasons known only to him, pulled up all of his wheat a week before harvest and threw it away. He wanted instead to grow a fruit he'd seen in a painting as a child. The plants were sourced from the Island, where the climate is completely different. They would not grow in the Valley. Moreover the cuttings he brought back had Mosaic virus on them, and it spread across to neighboring farms. Mr. Stainbourn was burned to death by an angry mob and the family descended back into poverty. Warren however kept the land and when he grew up was able to return it to an arable state. His wheat farming business is going well, but he is ambitious and wants to expand. He wants to invest in larger tracts of land and buy more farming equipment. He needs to hire more laborers and build facilities in which they can live. But the price of wheat is highly unstable. One harvest it's up, the next it's down. And this makes it extremely difficult for him to plan for the future. Pathologically afraid of financial failure as he is, he lays out these complaints in hushed tones to a trusty friend. Little does he know that the shrewd Alan Lysts, hidden by a large white pillar, are able to listen in on his conversation. Their financial brains start ticking and that evening instead of going home to their wives – both named Sylvia, both pregnant – they go to their offices and, as is their wont, hatch a scheme.

By sunrise the brothers have come up with a concept known as futures. For the scheme to work they will need the buy-in of the baker and the wheat farmer, and they believe they can help bring about stability in both of their trades. Warren Stainbourn – or any farmer for that matter – can secure the right to sell a fixed quantity and quality of their produce on a specified day in the future at today's market price. On the other end the baker can secure the right to buy a fixed quantity and quality of produce on a specified date at the agreed price. Both the baker and the farmer can now make more informed financial decisions knowing in advance how much they will be receiving or paying respectively. The Lyst brothers of course will take a small fee for facilitating the transaction. And everybodys a winner.

They invite Warren Stainbourn to their offices for a meeting. Taking great care of course not to offend the highly prickly man, and making certain they don't mention that they overheard him nattering in the pub, they lay out their proposal. Wheat is expensive at the moment, and Stainbourn is eager to lock in at the current price. They then call up the baker and lay the proposal on the line for him too. He realizes that the price of wheat is currently above average for the year, but he's heard a rumor that Banksy is planning on firing up the mint and letting new coins into circulation. He knows from studying his history books that this could well bring about inflation and push up the price of wheat. He thinks he's getting himself a bargain. Both baker and farmer put down a ten percent deposit as proof of their will to make good on the deal, and the contract is signed.

As it happens the baker, Ralph Dough, was correct and prices do go up slightly. But the price change was minor and Stainbourn is not perturbed. It certainly enabled him to plan with more accuracy and he's in the process of sourcing a new plot of land, and buying more equipment.

Suppliers and buyers in various trades soon notice the benefits of this futures system and the market grows rapidly. And again, it's not long before a new profession arises: professional futures traders. The Lyst brothers, and David Buysell, actively encourage these speculators as they bring liquidity to the market and help facilitate smooth transactions. The traders understand that in a simple futures agreement the seller is going short and the buyer going long. The speculators therefore try to take market conditions into consideration and if they think prices will go up they go long, and if they think prices will go down they go short. Of course they always need to offset their contracts before the date at which they expire, lest they should be forced to take delivery of something they don't need or sell something they don't have.

Because the professional futures traders need only put down a ten percent deposit in order to own a full-size futures contract, they begin to refer to themselves as, 'having leverage'. For example, if ten tons of wheat currently trades for 100 gold coins, a trader can buy the full contract by only putting down a ten percent deposit, i.e. 10 gold coins. But should the value of the wheat double in price, he will be able to sell the contract for 200 gold coins, and take the full profit. So by only putting up 10 gold coins, in the end he can walk away with a profit of 190 coins. It also means that a trader with a massive appetite for risk can enter into ten futures contracts for the mere price of the goods secured by one. The profits he stands to make if things go in his favor are astronomical. On the contrary however, should the price of the wheat decrease by just 10 percent, he will lose his entire investment. While it is always possible to double one's money or lose it all in any investment, this 'leveraged' aspect of futures trading means that one's profits or losses can be both massive and sudden in comparison with all other investment types. It is not a game for the faint of heart.

In the early days there are few if any who play such risky games and things seem to be going well, especially for the Stainbourns who have come some way in regaining their family's lost status. But then the price of wheat suddenly begins to rise. Speculators start buying up more contracts as they watch the price going up, and this pushes it up even higher. Warren Stainbourn is convinced that the market is making a mistake, especially given the fact that several new farms have recently been acquired by young startup farmers and are set to come into production soon. Obviously the market doesn't know about this, and some kind of mania, not logical deduction, is driving these prices. He is very happy to buy a contract to sell at this price and locks himself in for some big gains. But before he's able to leave his house for the market, his son Jeffry, only nineteen years old, stops him and explains that this is their chance to regain their family's fame and fortune, to forever silence those who laugh at them. They will never again see prices like this, and they must seize the moment. Why not trade two contracts instead of one, and before the next harvest comes they will find some new land and double their yield. After all, it's planting season now. Something tells Warren that this is not right, but his son persists and in the end he relents and enters into two contracts to sell.

They manage to acquire a tract of land, and plant their seeds. Long before harvest season they watch as the price starts to come down, and every night they devote ten minutes to patting one another on the back. Right on time, the crop they planted in their original plot starts to come up through the soil, but the crop in the new land does not. A day passes, two, three, and eventually they accept that something is awfully wrong. They take their spades and attempt to unearth the seeds. That day in the beating sun, they discover that the seeds have some kind of infection and are dying in the soil. That night back at their house Mrs. Stainbourn pulls down her husband's dusty family tree and lays it out in front of him. She says that for long she has feared this may well be the case. But now she knows for certain. The Stainbourns must carry a jumping gene and that's why the son in every second generation is a moron.

The Stainbourns are doomed.

A hurricane passes through the Valley and wipes out several neighboring wheat farms. Luckily their farm is spared, but the price of wheat starts to climb and soon passes its previous highs. In an attempt to help stabilize the Valley's economy Banksy runs a round of coin minting and allows more money to go into circulation. Against his intentions, much of the money finds its way onto the stock market, and speculators wishing to cash in on the ever rising price of wheat continue to buy up wheat futures, further driving up the price.

In order to make good on their promise the Staibourns are forced to sell their second plot of land and all the farming equipment. Using their home and original land as surety they are able to secure a loan from Milligan's bank. They plan to buy the wheat from a nearby farmer whose crop was spared. But the opportunistic farmer attempts to charge them more than the already high market price, and Warren is unable to pay.

The date for delivery comes and Stainbourn defaults. In accordance with a new law he is allowed to choose between incarceration and transportation. He chooses to be deported and the next day waves goodbye to his tearful wife and son as he sails off to a faraway, island continent. He arrives there two months later. All the other deportees are called Bruce. They all have big knives. In order to fit in, he changes his name to Bruce Stainbourn and marries a woman called Sheila. In accordance with the customs of the land, they call their firstborn son Bruce.

—◦ XII ◦—

FROM GOLD STANDARD TO FIAT

In which money does not stink but stinks for the Valley.

Our Valley goes from success to success and increasing numbers of outlying areas accede to it. Numerous wars are fought, battles lost and won. Leaders die and leaders are born, roads stretch ever further, and ships sail on to new horizons. The Cheesemakers maintain independence from the Valley whilst retaining their position as one of the Valley's chief trading partners. The Island too maintains its independence, and the three forge a multi-decade non-aggression pact. The Cheesemakers and the Island people find themselves in constant wars with other powers and are continually forced to borrow money from their own citizens as well as from foreign powers and foreign banks. After witnessing the success of the Valley's central bank in securing funding and lowering the rate at which the government could borrow, the other states in turn adopt similar systems with similarly successful results.

The Banksy family continues to control the Valley's central bank. With traders constantly having to travel great distances to do business, Banksy V has radically extended the ideas of his distant ancestor – Banksy II, the pariah – who gave paying clients the chance to deposit their gold in his bank in exchange for promissory notes. He has recently introduced a domestic policy whereby he is gradually taking all the gold coins out of circulation. He has melted many of them down and stores the bars in his bank's vaults. Alongside his old and much used coin mint he has opened a printing press in which he prints paper money. This money goes into circulation and is used by the citizens for transactions. However, the paper is accepted and maintains its value because, on the note there is a written and signed pledge that Banksy himself will hand over, to the bearer, the stated amount in gold should they so request it. Banksy has determined that one ounce of gold is valued at ten single denomination notes, or Vims, as the Valley currency is commonly known. This system is ingeniously self-regulating, for should Banksy be tempted to abuse his power and issue too many paper notes he would run the risk of causing their value to decrease in relation to gold on the open market. Should citizens grow wise to his ways they could arbitrage the difference. He knows that some shrewd citizens might exchange gold for notes on the free market and then take the notes to the bank and use them to reclaim gold. For example should Banksy be tempted to issue twenty notes for every ounce of gold in his safe, the market value of these notes could drop in relation to gold. Shrewd citizens would be able to swap one ounce of gold for twenty Vims, then take the Vims to the bank and exchange them for two ounces of gold. It is therefore in Banksy's best interest to keep the ratio constant and honest, and this system proves itself remarkably effective at keeping prices constant and inflation close to zero.

As the central banks on the Island and in the Cheesemaker nation secure their respective positions of power, the central bankers begin holding regular meetings in which they discuss the future of finance. With warfare increasingly less prevalent, their primary concern is maintaining a stable monetary regime, and in this regard Banksy is the acknowledged guru. With inter-societal monetary exchange on the rise, this system that has come to be known in the Valley as 'The Gold Standard', is soon adopted by the other central banks.

The three powers sign an historical agreement known as the Valley-Island-Cheesemakers (VIC) Pact. The VIC Pact states that each central bank will only issue as many paper notes as they are able to back with physical gold. Besides the citizens' ability to self-enforce the standard, each central bank vows to make its vaults open to inspection by the other powers. As all the economies are growing, they will be entitled to expand their official central bank gold reserves and their corresponding paper issuance each year in proportion to their economic expansion. Each currency will be pegged to the other and trade at a ratio of 1 to 1 to 1.

The central bankers and their boards are in constant communication with one another and meet annually: the location rotates. At their meeting, known as the Valley-Island-Cheesemakers Annual Bankers' Convention (with the difficult to pronounce acronym VICABC), the bankers present all available economic data from the previous year. Provided that none of the data is in contention, the respective banks receive permission to increase their gold reserves to a level appropriate to the expansion and thereafter issue the corresponding amount of new currency. For example if a given economy has grown by five percent, the central bank will be allowed to increase its gold reserves by five percent and allow five percent more currency into circulation. This system ensures that there is always appropriate liquidity in the societies to enable both large scale projects and day to day transactions. There is no shortage of gold on the free market, held by private banks, and in government coffers because of the massive mining operations of the past that flooded the markets with gold.

For over a decade this system works amazingly well, and bankers, governments, and citizens are mostly content. There is mild price deflation because there is always slightly less money in circulation than is needed by traders, banks and citizenry. As a result of this people are happy to leave their money in banks, or stuff it in their mattresses. This money hoarding behavior restricts economic expansion because wealth holders are less likely to pour their money into risky business ventures. After all they can generate good low risk real returns by doing nothing. Each year, with the same amount of money, they can buy more goods than they could the year before. Banksy believes these problems, however, are mild in comparison to run away inflation and other economic and social ills.

But then the first complaints arise. They come from a newly elected Island central banker, an eccentric man by the name of Primitus Prick. He has a wispy moustache, is fond of spectacles and uses a black cane, though those who know him well say he is perfectly capable of walking without one. He insists that the Island is undergoing a time of increasingly rapid expansion and it does not make sense for them to have to wait until the end of the year to increase their gold reserves and issue more currency. If they predict a booming year, they should be able to issue the currency in advance to enable them to facilitate this growth.

He paces up and down the conference room, tapping his stick on the table and says to his fellow bankers, 'honorable gentlemen! Money is a tool that enables society to function smoothly. It is to human civilization as water is to plants.

Does it make sense to first plant a hundred new acres of crop one year and then the following year acquire the water necessary to make them grow? By the time you bring the water the seeds may well have died in the soil, and even if they have not, you have lost a year of crops that could have been used to raise a farm of pigs that could have fed a team of men that could have built new irrigation lines to bring the water faster. Learned gentlemen, does it not make infinitely more sense to secure your water needs before you plant the seeds?'

Our Valley's esteemed banker, the great Banksy, insists that Mr. Prick does not understand the true nature of money and that his words are dangerous and misleading. He maintains that orderly development and honest monetary control is preferable, even if it appears to stifle growth. After all, he maintains, there is an inherent limit to how much growth a society can sustain, and a massive burst of growth in a short period will mean a period of volatility and stagnation or contraction thereafter.

But Banksy's speech is not enough to curb the rising enthusiasm amongst the bankers for this new idea and so it is agreed that banks should be allowed to increase their gold reserves and money base in advance of the new year and thus propel economic expansion.

But this is only the beginning of Primitus Prick's cunning plan. He enters into secret talks with the Island's leader, Dr. Tony Stiff – a firebrand youth leader in his student days, and a fierce nationalist – regarding the future of the Island's finances. Prick and Stiff agree that they've never much liked the Valleyians anyway. Their food smells bad and they talk too loudly. This gold standard agreement is not going to last, Prick says, and the first country to realize this and go off the standard will have a powerful first player advantage. Prick

77

tells Stiff that without warning he should appear before parliament and the country and announce that they have abandoned the gold standard. They will inform the Valley and the Cheesemakers via their envoys in those countries. It's not difficult to convince Stiff of this scheme. He drops the bomb and they revalue their currency downwards to one third of its previous value. They announce that their currency – the Isle – will no longer be convertible outside of the Island. The first Devaluing Wars, DW1, as they later become known as, have begun.

As Prick predicted, this move indeed gives the Island a valuable first player advantage. Completely taken by surprise as they are, the Valley is not able to respond effectively. With the Isle suddenly devalued, Valleyian importers cannot resist the temptation to use their now mighty Vims to import massive quantities of cheap Island goods that soon flood the Valley.

Prick and Stiff refuse to step down, insisting that their cause is just and that the Valley was exploiting them by forcing them to keep their currency pegged at an artificially high standard. Their plan has large-scale support within the Island as well, as it causes the local export industry to boom.

Vims pour into the Island. Although the Isle is no longer internationally convertible, Prick needs to ensure that its value relative to the Vim remains weak. In order to do this, he carries out large-scale smoke and mirrors operations wherein he issues new Isles and uses them to buy his own Vims. This pushes up the value of the Vim. As traders however still have a need to use Vims, should they start desiring them too much and driving up their value to the point that it passes the 3:1 ratio determined by Prick, he will use the Vims that he bought with the Isles he printed to buy back the Isles. That will cause the Isles to appreciate (increase in value).

As Banksy has not yet gone off the gold standard, Prick is able to swap some of his Vims for gold. And he does.

Banksy calls an emergency meeting with the Cheesemakers. Their central banker Franz Sharpe explains that the same thing is happening to them. Their currency – the Gouda – has been flowing into the Island and Prick is using his reserves to purge them of their gold. They agree that they must go off the gold standard at once. They send envoys to deliver the message directly to Prick, and assure him that if he so much as sends someone around to try and swap currency for gold, they will strap the man to a large wheel of cheese and roll him off a cliff.

Prick – a wholly unreasonable man – proclaims publicly that this is a massive injustice. Stiff goes so far as to call it an unprovoked act of war. The two men issue a declaration to this affect. Thankfully good taste prevails and they use their first names when signing it into law. The Primitus Tony Declaration (PTD) declares that they will do anything in their powers to protect their foreign and domestic trade interests from the unjust policies of foreign powers. Already currency manipulators of note, the two men get to work in devaluing their currency even further. They print massive amounts of Isles that they sell on the open market.

The other two powers respond. They fire up their printing presses and start selling their currencies and buying up the others. The Islanders have a head start and manage to stay in pole position in what becomes a destructive competitive devaluation race. It brings massive instability to the currency markets, and plays havoc with international trade.

The Valley then decides to up the game, and goes against its own long-term policy of free trade and places heavy import duties on all goods that come from the Island. The Cheesemakers do the same, and the Island retaliates by placing import duties on goods coming from the other two nations. Relations between the countries are extremely tense, and talk of war dominates newspaper headlines and barroom chatter.

—∘ XIII ∘—

THE GREAT DIVERGENCE

Where power shifts faster than tectonic plates.

Long before DW1 began The VIC countries had been in fierce and constant competition with one another. This evidently led to destructive encounters but had also the positive affect of fostering a spirit of one-upmanship: a lust to outperform and outdo. Their very identities became forged through the desire to outshine their neighbors.

In this fierce competition it is, above all, the institutions they have developed over the centuries to which they must turn. In all the VIC societies these are now complex and highly developed, and not only is there inter-country competition, but also fierce and constant rivalry amongst these very institutions within the countries. The governments do not have complete control over their districts any more than the large businesses, stock markets or banks. In some instances private families come to hold as much, if not more sway than the rulers themselves, and individuals are able on occasion to rise above the circumstances of their birth. Some believe that this possibility is what drives individual citizens and hence the success of these countries. Others believe it is their good fortune in geography and their access to natural resources.

Some say that the institutions themselves are better than those of nations outside of the VIC group, and there are even those – this idea is particularly popular amongst the Cheesemakers – who believe that the VIC people are racially superior. At this time in history none of these claims are easily testable or falsifiable, and they will remain contentious issues for centuries to come. What we do know is that at some point the VICs began to develop at a pace that outstrips that of all other nations.

Traders from the Valley had first noticed those sailing ships with crimson flags centuries ago, and exploration task teams that went on land came back with stories of civilizations as advanced or more so than their own. But due to the vast geographical distances between them, they hadn't developed serious trade relations. As the VICs advanced however, and their navigation techniques improved, they were able to travel with increasing ease to these distant lands. Although this had not been the case centuries before, when they arrived now, their technology was far superior to that of the local inhabitants. Their records reflected that the people with the crimson flags had once been better off economically than they were, but now they appeared to have fallen behind. This meant that the VICs could negotiate from a position of strength, and this they intended to do. The VIC countries were already wealthy, but from this point onwards they grew significantly wealthier. All interactions between themselves and the crimson-flag people (and other non-VIC nations), were biased towards themselves. In many cases they extracted large quantities of natural resources from them without paying anything like what they would have considered fair market prices. They forced the people to work for them, and in some cases enslaved them. They claimed that their superior force was the justification for the use of it. Of course there were those who were against this exploitative behavior, but for the most part traders were as happy to profit, as armies were to enforce their king's rules.

Once the VICs had gained this upper hand the wealth of the average citizen grew rapidly and then exponentially in relation to that of the non-VIC citizens. The unbalanced nature of the interactions of course had the opposite effect on the non-VICs, and their once prosperous and healthy societies underwent long and sustained periods of decline. Alan Lyst V in fact, once estimated that the average VIC was roughly 17 times wealthier than the average non-VIC. The wealth constantly reinvested in the VIC societies led to further industrial and cultural development and after several generations the average Vician – as they came to be known – knew virtually nothing about the non-Vicians, other than that they were poor. In the best of cases, they viewed them with pity and veiled contempt, and in the worst of cases with open revulsion and unveiled hatred. That a non-Vician was capable of making any kind of contribution towards society was a laughable idea, and so puppet-governments were put in place and the inhabitants of the countries lived under Vician laws.

The non-Vician societies become bones of contention amongst the Vics. All realized the enormous economic potential of these 'colonies' as they were known, and were willing to devote considerable financial and military resources to guard them.

Long-standing disputes over colonies flare up as the DW1 conflict intensifies. The world is now poised on the brink of war, and the Cheesemakers send a delegation to The Valley. They are worried that the Island is considering an attack and want to ensure that they can rely on the Valley to stand by them in such a military conflict. The envoy, a man named Constantine Flower, is en route home after signing a mutual-protection pact in the Valley Capital when a deranged Islander – an ex-soldier who had spent many years in the colonies – jumps from a tree into the envoy's carriage. He is wielding a large axe and takes great pleasure in driving it into Flower's forehead. The Island leadership refuses to denounce this attack, and two days later announce that the killer, Frank Marbles, has been inducted into the Hall of Greatness(HOG). The Cheesemakers consider this the ultimate insult, and an act of war. As it took place within the Valley's borders, Rich IX takes it as a personal insult. Furthermore, in accordance with the mutual-protection pact that had just been signed, the government is bound to take military action. The Mighty War begins.

The war rages for many years and thousands and millions of Vicians and non-Vicians are slaughtered. The war subsides for some time, but brings with it awful bouts of hyperinflation and widespread poverty. Resentment and anger at this new and awful state of affairs leads to a further, and even more widespread and destructive war. At the height of what becomes known as The Mighty Mighty War, the whole world is involved. It is so devastating that entire nations are obliterated. In the dying days of the war Banksy VIII is returning from one of the colonies when his ship, filled with gold, is hit by an Island U-Boat. Within moments the ship is standing at ninety degrees and sinking into the dark sea. It is believed that Banksy's second to last words are, 'I will never meet my son.' His wife had given birth just days before. His last words, so legend has it are, 'I will never again see my gold.'

Should he have been in a sounder state of mind, he may have taken comfort in the fact that his watery tomb was to be a gold lined one. It was not the fate of that ship to return to the Valley. And the gold, many believe, still lies, with Banksy's bones at the bottom of the ocean.

—✎ XIV ✎—
PWOS-NOM-FOR

The perfect currency system that was not.

Unlike the ship that was to become Banksy's watery grave, many treasure-laden vessels make it intact to the Valley during the course of the Mighty Mighty War. As they are the most powerful and wealthy amongst the VIC nations, and manage to a large extent to avoid the devastation of the fighting, the Valley is relied on to manufacture weapons and perform various services for countries around the world. During the MM War the Valley refuses to accept payment in paper currency: the fate of the various issuing nations is yet to be decided, and so the yellow metal itself is preferred. Those countries less endowed with gold are able to pay using other valuable commodities such as oil or platinum. Thus during the course of the MM War, massive quantities of commodities arrive in the Valley. Rich is particularly happy to see his vaults filling up with gold.

The peace finally comes. The Island and her allies are defeated, and the Valley, the Cheesemakers and their allies emerge victorious. It is agreed that the war has wreaked enough damage on all parties and punishment is not as important as forging a new way forward.

A worldwide monetary alliance must be drawn up. It will include not only the victorious parties, but also the vanquished. It will be worked out over the course of several weeks and signed in a banquet hall in the woods of Rich's Bretton Estate. The leaders of the countries and their respective central bank governors are all present. Rich of course is representing the Valley. With the death of Banksy VIII, and Banksy IX far too young to take up the position, a well-respected young economist Bob Note has been given the job of central banker. The Cheesemakers are represented by their wartime leader, Franz Cream. Albertus Skim is still serving as central bank governor. Tony Sharpe committed suicide at the end of the war and the Island now has a new leader, Martin Shovel. Primitus Prick still heads up their central bank. There are also numerous other minor countries present at the signing. They all sit together at a large round table. The victors eat caviar and lobster. The Island people are given macaroni and cheese.

The leaders want their system to be taken very seriously and believe that the more official the name sounds, the more seriously it will be taken. Thus after much debate they settle on the name Post War Official System with No Official Mechanism For Official Revaluation – PWOS-NOM-FOR.

Unfortunately, some feel that the excessive use of the word 'official', undermines its effectiveness. A well respected acronym consultant, Philip. P. Tightandshort, explains that in the view of The Ultimate Literal School of Acronymology (TULSOA) no single word should be used more than once in an acronym. The Cheesemakers object to this and point out that their mint MUFM – Mint Used For Minting, has been around for several centuries, and is widely respected. Tightandshort points out that the second time the word Mint is used it's in its 'ing' form. The argument rages on for days and the leaders get sidetracked, worrying more about whether or not the word official appears too many times in PWOS-NOM-FOR and not noticing that the real problem with the Post War Official System with No Official Mechanism For Official Revaluation, is that it has no official mechanism for official revaluation of currencies.

In the end they fire Tightandshort and sign the PWOS-NOM-FOR into law. Disagreement over the name aside, there is general consensus on many issues. All the powers want to avoid the problems of the pre-war free-floating currency days. Competitive devaluation, or as the political commentator and former Ironic acronymologist David Biglips called it, 'a race to the bottom', was destructive to the economies of all those involved. For the countries to go back to a traditional gold standard in which each central bank would expand its own supply in line with its economic expansion, is not a viable option. Both the Island and the Cheesemakers, as well as the other minor powers involved in the agreement have extremely sparse reserves, whilst the Valley is sitting on more than seventy percent of the world's known above-ground gold. It is therefore decided that the Valley will issue a gold backed Vim. The Vim will then serve as the currency against which all other currencies are valued. The countries will set their currencies at roughly pre-war levels, and the Valley will pledge that other countries may swap their Vims for gold. Citizens of the Valley however, are not granted the same privilege: their Vims are not redeemable for gold.

As the recovery rate and strength of the various economies going forward is so difficult to estimate, a clause is written into the agreement that states that countries will have the right and or obligation to a once-off revaluation of their currencies. Biglips and several other 'dissident commentators' do in fact point out that this clause in the PWOS-NOM-FOR is not clearly defined – is it a right? an obligation? who will enforce it? They worry that trade imbalances may come about if countries attempt to exploit this uncertainty and keep their currencies unnaturally low. But due to the bickering over the name, no one pays them any attention.

Gold is pegged at 35 Vims per ounce: the pre-war price. As the Valley has massive reserves, and mining has reopened (it closed during the war, as it was seen as a non-essential operation) the powers estimate that there will be plenty of gold available to help finance world growth for the next several decades. Governments thinking several decades in advance is in itself an historical event. With the signing of the agreement the Valley's central bank becomes in effect the central bank of the world, and the Vim the world's reserve currency.

At first the Valley's economy is far more powerful than any of the other major powers, and for well over a decade they record a trade-surplus: more goods flow out of the Valley than into it, and hence there is a genuine and honest demand amongst their trading partners for Vims: so much so that there is a constant shortage, making Vims in effect more valuable than the gold by which they are backed. During these years the standard of living of the average Valleyian is constantly rising. They build big houses, buy fast cars, and eat lots of hamburgers.

But after about fifteen years – the time it takes for them to rebuild their industries – the other powers are able to start competing more effectively in the international market. The Islanders and the Cheesemakers still have a relatively low standard and cost of living, and their labor – priced internationally – is cheaper. Very soon, both the

89

Cheesemakers and the Islanders are exporting more than they are importing, and their products start flowing into the Valley. When the situation was in reverse – in the previous decade – it acted as a kind of shock therapy for the countries to get their industry into order. If they wanted to be able to pay for the products they imported they had to start exporting. But now the Valley doesn't feel the same shock. Because of the Vim's status their trading partners continue to accept it because they can use it to buy commodities, or anything they desire, from anywhere in the world. They (the Valley) are thus not forced into improving their industry or lowering their costs.

Bob Note remains in control of the central bank. Banksy IX is still at university, but has already gained a reputation as an outspoken critic of the current system. He believes that it is not the fault of the Valley that these trade imbalances are occurring. He constantly refers back to the PWOS-NOM-FOR documents and insists that, in keeping with the spirit of the agreement, the other countries are obliged to revalue the currencies upwards. The trading ratios between their currencies was set just after the Mighty Mighty War, when the Cheesemakers and Islanders' industries had been all but destroyed. But now that they are able to compete again it is not fair that they undercut the Valleyians by keeping their currencies artificially weak. What's more, he claims, global expansion has necessarily lead to an increased demand for money, and as the Vim is the world's reserve currency, and can be used to pay for international transactions, it has necessitated a loser monetary policy on the part of Note and the reserve bank. Though Note agrees with much of what Bansky says, he asks Rich if he can do something to silence him. He is afraid that young Banksy is pointing out a major flaw in the system. With the Vim as the reserve currency of the world and thus constantly in demand, there is no way that their real gold supply will be able to keep up with the monetary expansion necessary to service the entire world's growth.

Banksy Jr. is brought to heel, but the trade imbalances continue. Vims flow out of the Valley and goods flow in, and though Valley industries are unable to compete, the Valleyians continue to live well, paying for cheap imported goods with their special reserve currency. Vims start to pile up in the vaults of their trading partners'. A headline in The Daily Dairy – a right leaning newspaper in the Cheesemaker's Land – reads 'Vims, Vims, Everywhere! Hold or Swap? We like Gold!'

David Biglips, now in his late sixties, starts speaking out about the problems that he insists he warned about when the PWOS-NOM-FOR was signed. As is to be expected, the Cheesemakers and Islanders start swapping a portion of the Vims they acquire each year for gold: everyone in their countries agrees that it's vital to hedge against the inflow of this single currency. The Valley keeps to their promise and each year, ships over a small amount of gold to the Cheesemakers and the Islanders. Over the course of the next decade and a half the imbalances reach disturbing levels, and the other powers are increasingly anxious about getting their hands on the Valley gold, and each year trade in larger and larger portions of their Vims.

The Cheesemakers and Islanders are clearly losing faith in the Vim, but both are afraid of cashing in too many Vims in one go, should they spook the other, or the lesser powers, and cause a rush on the Valley's central bank. This could potentially cause an overnight collapse of their currency standard: not something they want to see happen. Nevertheless, during this time almost two thirds of the gold flows out of the vaults of the Valley and into the others' banks.

The markets become increasingly unstable, and gold, priced on the open market continues to rise. During previous – country-by-country – gold standards, the issuing authority was self-regulated by the population, who could, if the market price of gold differed greatly from the price pledged by the bank, arbitrage the difference. Under the PWOS-NOM-FOR however, that cannot be done, because Valley citizens are not able to swap their Vims for gold. As was the case with all previous monetary regimes (and most things that governments are involved in) the most important thing is maintaining the appearance of order and legitimacy. If the free-market is deciding that gold is really worth more than the 35 Vim price set during The PWOS-NOM-FOR, the illusion of a stable currency begins to fade.

Central bankers from the VIC countries – Note, Skim and Prick – meet on the Island one rainy evening and pledge to do everything in their powers to keep the price of gold on the market down. Firstly they will give their alliance an acronym: NOSP. Note gets to use two letters from his name because the Valley has the largest economy, and it makes the acronym pronounceable. With the confidence that having an acronym brings they act with force and determination, and start selling vast quantities of gold on the open market to try and drive the price down and rescue their currency system. This seems at first to have its desired affect, and NOSP agrees to keep it up. A transfer of gold away from the central bankers and governments is a hefty price to pay, but it's infinitely better than watching their currency system collapse.

The Valley continues to spend vast quantities of Vims, which continue to pile up en-masse in the vaults of the Cheesemakers and the Islanders. The other countries accuse

Note of being far too liberal with his monetary policy and insist that he's allowing too many Vims into circulation. Note continues to accuse them of deliberately keeping their currencies undervalued, and insists – in private meetings with Rich – that he has no choice but to try to devalue their currency by printing more of it, if they want to compete in the international market.

'Was this not what the agreement was put in place to prevent?' Rich asks.

'Yes it was' says Bob Note. 'And we thought we would win out by having international goods priced in our currency. But the other countries have abused us, and used our money to pay for things. It's so unfair!' he says and begins to sniffle. 'I've had to accommodate them by printing and printing and printing. Do you think I want to print? And now they're coming for my blood. It's not fair!' He almost bursts into tears, but Rich manages to calm him down.

NOSP continues selling gold on the open market, but the Island and the Cheesemakers become increasingly frustrated with trying to defend a system that they no longer see as working in their favor. The Valley is forced to hand over more and more gold each year to pay off their deficit. In order to try and hang on to some of their reserves they devalue the Vim, from 35 Vims per ounce to 38 then 38 to 42, but still they are being purged.

One day Rich announces that he will be giving a press conference at which he will deliver a very important message. Journalists from around the world gather in the briefing room. He comes out and stands behind the podium. Cameras flash as he wipes sweat off his face. The world is waiting for his statement.

He breathes in deeply, shouts, 'We're off!' and runs backstage before anyone can ask any questions.

It's up to one of his aides to explain that by, 'we're off', he means off the gold standard.

Biglips writes an opinion piece that can be basically summed up as, 'I told you all so!' He claims that the Valley has – though it is not officially recorded as such – defaulted.

Whatever they wish to call it, this bold move sends shocks through the world's financial markets. Contrary to the predictions of one of the world's foremost economists at the time, Simon Counter, the price of gold does not decline to its industrial value. Instead it rises, then rises more and more and then some more.

—☙ XV ☙—

POST PWOS-NOM-FOR

In which the foretold but not foreseen comes to pass.

Of course this is not the first time in Valley history that the government has chosen to turn its back on the gold standard, and embrace the floating or fiat system. But this time there's a twist. The world comes un-pegged from gold but not from the Vim. The Vim remains as the world's reserve currency, and the Valley's Central Bank remains, essentially, the central bank of the world. It is said by some insiders that Note can be seen at night pacing the walkways of his mint, looking down at the printing press, a sick and maniacal gleam in his eyes. He has concluded, some say, that the Banksy family will never again take control of the central bank. For Note has become somewhat sick with power and believes that his is unlike that of any man who has ever strolled this earth. The value of fiat currency – he understands well – is not determined by anything other than supply and demand. And as long as the Vim remains the reserve currency of the world and can be used to buy commodities on the international market, there will always be demand, and the Vim will always remain relatively strong. In the past, as the de-facto master of the world's printing press, he was limited in his power. If he over-printed, those pesky Cheesemakers and anal Islanders, would bring back handfuls of his paper and demand he hand over his gold: and everyone knows that Note (just like the Banksy family before him) loves nothing more than gold. He had watched as his beloved treasure drained slowly from his vault and the stress was so awful it gave him ulcers in his stomach, and boils beneath his eyelids. His hair was falling out in patches, and he'd vomit in the mornings. He still has vast supplies of gold of course, and at night (he only sleeps for two hours a day) he lies down amongst it. But his mind is increasingly elsewhere. Gold is my wife, he says to a trusty aide, but the printing press is my mistress.

Even during the years of PWOS-NOM-FOR, international currencies were only indirectly pegged to gold. But since its demise they are now truly free-floating entities, fiat once again. They bring with them all the freedoms and all the problems of the previous fiat regimes. The sudden shock of switching from a quasi-gold-standard to a global fiat currency means that there is great instability in the currency markets for some time. In order to try and stabilize the local markets, Note increases the money supply. It works temporarily, but does not solve the problem. Rich however encourages him to keep up a liberal monetary policy. During the PWOS-NOM-FOR days the Valley fell behind the Cheesemakers and the Islanders in competitiveness, and in order to get the economy ticking again they need to be generous. Note agrees with Rich and they pursue what they refer to as an 'accommodative monetary policy'. They keep their interest rates at close to zero, and make money easily available to the bankers who in turn hand on the low interest rates to their customers. But as happened so many generations before in the Valley's infancy, an increase in money supply leads to an increase in prices. To try and combat the price increases Note issues more money and this further drives up the prices.

Banksy, who has now graduated from university and is running his own private equity firm, begins to make a name for himself as a pundit on television. He refuses to be drawn on one of the hottest debates of the day: will he seek appointment as the next central bank governor? Many believe it is his rightful place, but he says that what interests him is sound policy, not status. The Valley is in turmoil. Inflation is sitting at around ten percent per annum and this makes it impossible for businesses to factor in pricing accurately and hence they cannot make proper decisions. Households are being destroyed too. Inflation Machines (IMs) become extremely popular. Shops and restaurants have price tags with revolving numbers and each hour an employee winds the IM and ups the price. At the height of the inflation many outlets have to assign an employee to this task on a permanent basis. He turns the lever around and around and the prices go up and up. Across the Valley there is a spate of inflation killings, known in the news as SOIK. They generally happen in fast food outlets when someone takes too long to order from a menu. A customer standing behind them gets increasingly agitated as they watch the price going up. In a moment of blind rage they reach for a lethal object and murder the dawdler. In one particularly tragic event a wife beat her husband to death with a tray after he took fifteen minutes to decide whether he should upsize his meal.

The situation is made worse when citizens hear rumors of Bob Note's spendthrift wife Celine. Before the two hit the town for the night, Bob will ask her, 'how much do you think we'll need honey?' and then quickly fires off a round of notes on his printing press.

As in the past the inflation brings the Valley to its knees and ushers in an awful and savage recession. Unemployment rises and there are riots on the streets. Households that had become accustomed to an excellent standard of living are coming closer each day to living in poverty. Rich's legitimacy as a leader is constantly challenged, and he fears that there may be a full-blown revolution in the Valley. In order to curb the rising waves of violence and unrest Rich, instead of asking Note to reverse his policies, pressures him into keeping interest rates low, encouraging borrowing and increasing the money supply. He is convinced that if they can just get through this patch somehow, things will get better: somehow they must get better!

After half a decade of crippling inflation, Banksy IX – who has made a name for himself as a private financier – makes it clear that he has his mind set on reclaiming his family's central bank. He challenges Note to a debate on television, insisting that unless they manage to bring inflation under control, it will be the end of the Valley. The way things are, he says, businesses cannot hire and households cannot budget! This, he claims, is beyond disastrous for an economy: it is ruinous. He is the first to coin the phrase, 'The Great Inflation.'

At the same time Note begins to look increasingly disheveled. Celine leaves him, but keeps a spare key to the printing press room. He shows up late for press conferences, in unironed shirts and crumpled suits. His beard is unkempt and the cameras detect a reddish tone in his eyes. Some say that he has turned to the bottle. But in truth Note cannot sleep because at night he thinks he can see the ghost of Banksy strolling along the walkways of the central bank, looking down at the printing press. Some say the bank is truly haunted and others believe it is merely a projection of

Note's guilty conscience: his policy failures are manifest in the faces of the hungry that line up outside soup kitchens, in the look of the man whose house has been repossessed, in the eyes of the woman whose business has gone bankrupt. These images merge into the faceless form of Banksy I, and their cries mingle with Banksy's voice as he moans – *money is nothing. You cannot print our Valley back to life.*

On the night of the Great Debate, set to take place live on prime time television, Note fails to show up, and this is widely seen as an admission of defeat. Two days later Bob Note, on evening television, announces that he will be stepping down as the governor of the reserve bank. By the end of the week Banksy IX is officially sworn in. At his inauguration he explains to the Valleyians that things are going to get a lot worse before they get better. He insists that the path Bob Note was following was completely unsustainable, and that inflation must be brought under control before the Valley can return to prosperity. In order to do this, he announces that he will, and subsequently does, increase the interest rate to over 20 percent. Some accuse him of criminal behavior, and insist that this is usury. But he will not be swayed from his path and explains to Rich that tightening up the money supply is the only way to end the Great Inflation.

At first things do get worse. More businesses go under, and average citizens begin to demand the return of Note. Things were bad then, but not as bad as this. Banksy's critics – and there are many – say that he has lost touch with reality and that he is attempting to cure a problem that runs much deeper than monetary policy. But Banksy is convinced – and manages to convince Rich too – that inflation is purely and completely a monetary issue, and that once the excess has been worked out of the system things will return to normal.

The Valley continues down this path for several years, but eventually, as he promised he would, Banksy brings inflation under control. The Valley has been traumatized by the awful inflation and then the phenomenally high interest rates. But the experience has also awoken a healthy fear of debt and excess in the Valleyians. When the Valley starts to come back to life, it does so at a stable rate, and for the most part wise investment decisions are made. Stable prices mean that businesses can again begin to hire and Valleyians can again start to spend. Within a few years, the Valley is booming again!

But as some critics begin to note, there is a distinct cycle in business and economics. Some economists start referring to it as The Boom and Bust Cycle. As things start heating up, people are more and more willing to take on risk. Banks are happier to lend out money, and Banksy, delighted to see that his plans for healing the economy worked, decides that he must accommodate this new phase in growth. He continues to lower interest rates and some say that he turns into a new man entirely. He leaves his wife, Brimhilda Banksy nee Fisher and takes up with a young blonde woman named Annie. B. Spank. The two are seen around town, living the highlife. Banksy reestablishes his friendships with the men from his private banking days and they encourage him to constantly loosen up his monetary policy. He accommodates them, and soon history is forgotten, it simply vanishes. No one seems to remember the days of the Great Inflation. Banksy himself never even talks about it. These days it's all about boom and growth and more growth. The talk is of a new paradigm. The role of the central bank as a force for good has been established. With the right helmsman, it's agreed, financial disasters can be averted and perpetual growth and prosperity achieved.

But as the party rages night and day, mistakes from the past come creeping back, unnoticed by most. An excess of Vims means a constant outflow from the Valley. The Vims once again start collecting in the vaults of the Cheesemakers, the Islanders and the Valley's other trading partners. The Valley has become more competitive in terms of exports, but as the standard of living rises again, so do wages and the demands of the workers. They want their equal share of the wealth, and employers have to compete to keep workers. They raise wages and guarantee pensions and healthcare schemes. Much the same thing is happening on the Island and in the land of the Cheesemakers. The Islander's government has taken on an increasingly dominant role in their citizens' lives, paying pensions, unemployment benefits, medical care and childcare. Rich does not have such socially minded schemes and leaves many of these responsibilities to employers. All the same, the standard of living in all three countries continues to rise and the Valleyians increasingly struggle to import cheap goods from their trading partners. Although they do export goods, the vast majority of their economy is made up of domestic consumption. The Valleyians increasingly consider themselves the 'idea people' and the adders of additional value. They can design or improve, but others can do the dirty work of putting things together. But, ideas and designs are not enough. In order for the Valley to boom, people have to buy. Their shops must be filled with goods: if not their own, then those manufactured cheaply in another country. Spending means jobs and jobs mean spending. But cheap goods are increasingly hard to import and increasingly impossible to produce locally.

It seems that we're getting flashbacks from history. The Valley is unable to keep up its economic expansion. To prevent a recession or depression, Banksy does just what he used to accuse his predecessor of doing, and prints more money. He lowers interest rates and increases money supply. Inflation begins to creep back in. As prices go up, citizens cut back on spending, and businesses cut back on hiring. It looks as if the Valley is entering another depression.

Very possibly history may have played itself out in much the same way as it did in the past, and, with time and some pain, everything in the Valley would have gone back to normal. But this time something else happens: something that will change everything.

—๑ XVI ๑—

THE RISE OF THE CRIMSONS

In which power shifts, unlike continental drift, are reversible.

Remember the people of the Crimson Flag? Those whom our Valley's traders had first encountered in their earliest days and later exploited with glee? Since the end of the Mighty Mighty War, there has been little contact between the nations, and the people of the Crimson Flag have fallen further and further into poverty even as our Valley has grown richer and richer. The Crimson Flag people have been exposed not only to the exploitative ways of the Vicians, but have since come to live under consecutive repressive systems. Their own leaders have run totalitarian regimes that attempt to control every aspect of their citizens' lives. The Crimson society itself is as ancient or more so than the Vician societies, but many of the institutions that have revolutionized the Vics and propelled them forward have been ignored or rejected by the Crimson leaders.

For several decades a fat Crimson man named Big Boss 'Kitty Cat' Meow, rules with an incompetent iron fist and starves millions of his people to death. But when the fat man dies and his body stored in a large mausoleum in the centre of the capital, another man whose name no one in the Valley will ever remember or learn to pronounce, comes up with a plan. He wants to bring about large-scale reforms that attempt – in part – to emulate the successful aspects of the Vician societies and their institutions. In particular, his wants to de-regulate the markets and emulate the free-market models of the Vics. And, because he associates their usage with wealth creation, he decides to give his reform program an acronym. On the advice of a Valleyian based freelance Neoclassical acronymologist, he first comes up with the acronym and then finds the words to match it. He chooses the word POWER, and uses the words: People's Organization With Excellent Resources.

Because the Crimsons have for so long feared the free market ideas, they decide to try them out with caution and open up some special trade zones – known as POWER Zones – where they can try these policies out before introducing them to the whole country. As the man – whose name no one in the Valley knows (it's actually Sam Bigkick) – had predicted, free-markets work infinitely better than price-fixed markets. Soon, the test-zones are booming, and Bigkick and his party decide to import them into the rest of Crimson Land.

The sons of two of our Valley's most famous business families – Basket and Fisher – decide to take a gap year in Crimson Land, and whilst traveling start to sense that the political and social landscape of the ancient land is shifting. After decades of government intervention and price control, prohibition of private property ownership and militarily enforced state monopoly, things are starting to ease up, and markets are being set free. This impresses the two young capitalists, but they notice that most Crimson people can barely afford the food they need to feed their families. They are horrendously poor, far worse off than the average

Valleyian. In fact, they conclude that the divide between the two is even greater than when Alan Lyst made his calculations some century before. And to a bright capitalist this means one thing: they will, and indeed must work for low wages. The famous Basket/Fisher brains begin ticking. Calculations are made, drinks are drunk, and of course – because it is after all a gap year – Crimson women are seduced at industrial levels.

On their return to the Valley the two begin to draw up the blueprint of what will become the dominant trend of the decades that follow. The Fisher and Basket Enterprise has grown into a multi-national conglomerate that controls numerous enterprises and owns many brands. In the preceding decades they'd shifted their focus from fishing to manufacturing, and own factories that produce everything from frozen foods to clothes and common electrical appliances to luxury goods. They employ tens of thousands of Valleyians, but their profit margins have been steadily declining. At first paying their workers higher salaries had incredibly positive affects as it enabled the workers to be consumers of the products they created. But with time, the workers' unions have come to insist on inconvenient things like health care, and – without any consideration for the shareholder's at all – constantly demand higher wages. And then there's Rich's government that has caved in and granted minimum wage guarantees. This has driven up costs and driven down profits. But a minimum wage, they learn on their trip to the land of the Crimsons, is a relative concept.

After graduating from famous 'green-creeping-plants on the wall' universities and writing theses on the benefits of out-sourcing and internationalizing the work-force, they take over their fathers' companies and begin, what becomes known as 'the great off-shoring.'

They identify those workers with highly specialized skills and offer them attractive packages if they'll agree to move to Crimson Land. As for those who perform the more menial jobs they explain that it's nothing personal, but that they've found people who can do the same thing they can for a fraction of a fraction of the cost. One of the first factories they set up in Crimson Land is a watch factory, and in order to show their Valleyian one-time employees that there are no hard feelings, they give each one, on their last day of work, a golden watch. On the underside of these watches are the words that will one day inspire international awe, envy and disgust: Made in Crimson Land.

The process is simple enough. Factories are shuttered up and the land is sold off. New factories are then built in Crimson Land and local employees are hired and trained up. Of course all this moving requires money and the young men start tapping the banks and the stock markets. During the days of easy money in the Valley, many of the large banks had been borrowing at almost zero interest rates and hoarding the cash in anticipation of further financial difficulties or defaults. But now, with the dawning of this new age of possibility, the bankers are excited about putting their money to work: and the money begins to flow. It flows right across the world into Crimson Land, where it collects in many a nook and many a cranny. The Crimson people and their government are only too happy to welcome the Valleyians. They are happy to receive their Vims, because after all, the Vim never lost its status as the world's reserve currency, and so they can use it to buy goods that they need on the international market. Particularly, they can use it to pay for the massive quantities of oil they need to import into their country to help drive this sudden upturn in their economy.

Besides the gold watches, many products that once read Made in The Valley, now read Made In Crimson Land. They appear to be exactly the same, only they cost much less. Because they cost less, people are able to start buying them, and so the Valley's economy starts to awaken from the recent depression.

Basket and Fisher Enterprises have managed to slash their production costs, and it is inevitable that very soon everyone else wants to copy them. Outsourcing becomes the in-word, and factories are shuttered up by the thousand and re-opened in Crimson Land. Complex products that need numerous components will be set up all across Crimson Land, and the component parts will be pieced together there too. Sometimes the raw materials can be sourced within Crimson Land and sometimes they must be found in other regions. Wherever they may come from however, the Vim can be used to acquire them. The Valley is soon inundated with Crimson made products. But the Valleyians themselves are still very much involved in creating the products they consume. For example, a smart Valleyian will come up with an idea, like drawing a banana on the left pocket of a shirt. They will then pay other smart people to make large banners with the image of that banana on it, and hang those banners all over the big cities in the Valley. They will get famous people to say that they like wearing the shirts with the banana drawn on the left pocket, and soon the value of the banana image itself will be worth more than the material used to make it or the factories in which it is made. The people who draw the posters with the banana on them will make large sums of money which they will spend on the products they market and on other luxury items. And so the most extraordinary thing starts to happen. The Valleyians have realized that using their superior Vician thinking, they have once again managed to outwit the non-Vicians. They no longer have to work in dirty factories or do manual labor. They are the thinkers, the designers, the managers and visionaries. The Crimsons are the workers, and consuming foreign made goods at low cost is a fair reward for the Valleyians' enterprising spirit.

Banksy of course is delighted and he is known to run his printing press both day and night. Bansky makes Vims easily available to banks, and they in turn, are only too happy to lend them to ambitious young entrepreneurs. Loans are taken out and design teams and think groups are set up in The Valley, and factories are set up in Crimson Land. Vims flow in astronomic proportions towards Crimson Land and products continue to flow back into the Valley. Bigger and bigger shops are set up to store them, and more elaborate campaigns are designed to get people to buy them. All this leads to the Valley's cosmetic appearance constantly increasing and anyone who comes to visit can see that it is the greatest nation of all. When Rich's government needs money anyone and everyone is happy to lend it to them at low interest rates, and this enables them to further finance and support many great operations within and outside of their borders. They give loans to anyone who wants to study anything. They continue to build a massive army, larger than any the world has ever known. They are admired, loved, feared and hated. Our Valley has become greater than anyone could ever have dreamt, and in its slipstream the other Vicians fly.

In Crimson Land things are also going well. A social revolution is taking place. The enormous and ancient land that has for centuries been primarily a subsistence farming economy is turning into a manufacturing superpower. Hundreds, millions and finally hundreds of millions of people move away from their villages and head towards the cities where they can find work in the factories. Many of the factory workers learn about the Valley and the other Vician societies. They see images of them on television, read about them in magazines and wonder if one day they'll be able to live similar lives. Many of the workers are able to save up large sums of money and they use this money to invest in their children's education, and after a generation some of these children are able to travel over to the great Valley or the Island or the land of the Cheesemakers and study at their famous institutions and bring home their knowledge to the Crimsons.

The Crimsons' wealth steadily grows and their savings are constantly increasing. Their own domestic economy advances and they continue to improve their standard of living. They still admire the Vics, and still believe they have much to learn from them. They are after all the ones who first mastered many of the institutions – banks, central banks, bond markets and stock markets – that they are largely relying on to drive their economic revolution. In a different situation the Valley would have to constantly buy the Crimsons' local currency in order to pay for products from them. In order for them to do this they would have to sell massive quantities of goods. But because the Vims are the global reserve currency, they don't have to worry about those kinds of things. The Crimsons are happy to accept the billions and trillions of Vims that flow towards them in exchange for the products they manufacture. As the Vims build up they wish to put them to use, and decide to start investing in the bonds issued by Rich's government. They see these as a good financial investment, and also as a means of asserting their power in this new world. They know well that borrowers have to speak in a small voice when talking to their bankers.

Over the years and decades they continue to build up massive holdings of Vims, and keep over a trillion Vims worth of Valley bonds on their books.

For a while everything seems to be perfect, but to those who look a little closer they see a problem developing. And those who look even closer notice that the problem is not new. Over-valued currencies and under-valued currencies; trade deficits and surpluses. It all happened before during the DW1 and then again during PWOS-NOM-FOR days. Now the Valleyians insist that the Crimsons are keeping their currency – the Crimo – undervalued. As the trade deficit increases, few in the Valley consider the implications, but those who do point out the fact that the Crimsons are master currency manipulators. If Banksy's central bank used a bit of smoke and a few mirrors, the Crimsons have in the words of Banksy himself, 'an entire disco laboratory.' In actual fact the Crimsons' central banker – Small Cat 'Quite Cute' Meow – did his doctoral thesis on the DW1 days. He learned a lot from Primitus Prick, whom the Crimsons call Prick of the Island (POTI). In secret memos circulated only amongst Crimson Party members, they refer to their policy as the POTI Effect.

First of all, they do not allow their currency to be traded outside of their own country. Although their economy rises up rapidly through the ranks, the Crimo is not traded on the open currency market. Only a country that runs a massive trade surplus is able to do this of course, as they do not need to pay for any of their foreign currencies using Crimos, but instead acquire foreign reserves by accepting them as payment for exported goods.

The central bankers aim to keep the Crimo pegged to the Vim, and in order to do this they perform fantastical buy and sell operations within their borders. Within Crimson Land of course, there is a kind of international currency market, as businesses need to buy and sell Crimos, Vims and other currencies to carry out their international business transactions. All the major banks have large reserves of foreign currencies as a result of international traders' deposits. If the internal market begins to valuate the Crimo too highly for the Crimson government and central bankers' liking, then they issue new Crimo and use it to buy up Vims, thereby driving up the price of the Vim and knocking down the Crimo. Should the Crimo become too weak for their liking, they will use the Vims they earlier bought with their Crimo and buy Crimo, thereby driving up the price of the Crimo and knocking down the price of Vims. This is of course performed within the central bank. In the earlier days it was necessary to wheel the money from one corner of the safe to the other in order to change its value, but with the rise of technology they need only press a few buttons for the POTI effect to work.

Banksy calls this behavior deplorable, but there is nothing he can do to change it, and there are even some who say his real problem is jealousy. It seems that the Crimson central bankers may have even more power than he does.

THE GREAT PLEASURE BOAT BUBBLE

The offspring of easy money and stupid people.

Bubbles are a most intriguing thing. They have occurred throughout the history of The Valley and the other Vician societies, and since Crimson Land opened up, it too has experienced numerous bubbles. In fact, bubbles it seems, are an unfortunate and inevitable side-effect of human beings being, well, human.

This is how they work. Someone identifies a need in society and comes up with an idea on how to address it: this often includes the invention of some kind of new technology. The individual goes to the bank and asks the banker to lend him some money. If the banker considers his idea to be legitimate, he will lend him the money. If not, he will drag him out by his coat and throw him onto the street. If the banker does lend him the money and his idea is good, if his technology is truly innovative, his business will grow. In order to raise further finances he will list his company on the stock exchange, and a small handful of individuals, perhaps one of the Alan Lysts, will notice this company, be intrigued by the technology its using, recognize the company's prospects and buy its stock. If the company continues to do well the shares will rise and this will catch the attention of other investors. After they've noticed the price rising consistently for a period of time, they'll see the stock as a good bet and want to buy some for themselves, further pushing up the price. At the same time other entrepreneurs will notice that this new industry seems to be doing well. They'll draw up their own business plans and go to the bank to get a loan. The banker, noting that the sector is doing well, will be happy to give a loan to anyone who plans to operate in it. The new person then lists his company on the stock market and buyers clamber to get the shares, pushing the price up quickly. Soon, entrepreneurs who may have gone into something else, get word that everyone in this new sector is making money and so decide to drop their old plans and jump on board. They get a loan easily and their shares are snapped up. Every company operating in the sector continues to do well, and their share prices climb higher and higher and soon anyone with any spare money wants to get in on the action and invest in any company in the sector, regardless of whether its plans are sound or its products good. Banks are keen to make loans to businesses, entrepreneurs are keen to start businesses, investors want to profit, and soon the supply of the product or service that once had a legitimate purpose, massively outstrips the demand. The investors who bought shares in the first company realize that their value is now unrealistically high. If they sell them now, they'll be able to make a huge profit, and there are plenty of buyers. They sell, and walk away. Others begin to notice they're leaving and sell their shares too, and the value begins to drop. At first some of the latecomers see this as a good chance to buy more shares, but then the price drops more and then more. Eventually, the latecomers, who make up the majority of the buyers, realize they've paid more for their shares than they should have, and in a panic they all try to sell at the same time and the prices collapse. Some get rich, many get poor, and usually after the dust has settled something of actual value is left behind.

In the case of the famous railway bubble for example, at the height of the madness over half the Valley's inhabitants were involved in either building railway lines, sourcing materials needed to make railway lines, building trains or sourcing train material, building stations or sourcing the goods needed to build them. Most of those involved in the projects would invest their money in the stocks of companies involved. Those not directly involved, would likewise invest their money in railway companies. By the end there were thousands of kilometers of railway lines that would never serve any purpose. There were hundreds of companies that would go bankrupt and many who would lose their life savings. But, the mania left behind thousands of kilometers of train tracks, and these would forever benefit the citizens of the Valley.

But the great pleasure boat bubble brings only disaster. The reason for this was that the innovations of the recent years have not been in railways technology; they have not been in any technology. The innovations of the recent years have been in finance itself. And so when the bubble bursts it leaves nothing of any value in its wake.

The co-conspirators are the bankers, the brokers, the central bankers and the government. There is also a new group that plays their role too. Two Alans from the great Lyst empire have broken away from traditional investing and instead set up a new line of business called ratings services. What they do is look at any investment on offer and give it a rating anywhere from AAA to XXX. AAA means it is perfectly safe and no matter what happens, if you invested in it, your money will be safe. If it is rated XXX it is only for those with lots of money, very thick skins, or no brains. Their agency called Alan's and Alan's, is of vital importance, because it allows investors – particularly those who are responsible for money that absolutely must not be lost, like money in pension funds – to find the safest place to put it.

Pleasure boats have always been fashionable in the Valley. When a rich man or woman achieves a certain level of success, it is common for him or her to go out and buy a pleasure boat. The boat will have a beautiful deck, fine interiors, sleeping quarters, a sound system and some powerful engines. Of course these boats cost a lot of money and they were traditionally thus available only to the ultra rich. But as prosperity spread through the Valley and credit became increasingly easy to come by, more and more people were able to afford pleasure boats. If they couldn't pay for them upfront they could take out a loan. But the bankers still had to be careful about whom they gave these loans to. That is until the great revolution in credit and finance.

Rich XII states that everyone in the Valley is entitled to own a pleasure boat, and he will help ensure that the bankers enable this dream to become a reality. At this point in time two minor characters from earlier reemerge. They are the descendents of the men who pushed for the first ever fiat money system. They are born of immigrant parents who came to the Valley during one of its many booms. Their names are Frederico Prick and Benjamin Sharpe. They however do not have the tact of their Island ancestors and open up shop under the name Sharpe Prick's Bank. They advertize special, 'Pleasure Boat Loans'.

'Have you ever dreamt of owning a pleasure boat? Financial difficulties standing in the way of this dream? At Sharpe Prick's we believe that just because you can't afford a pleasure boat, doesn't mean you shouldn't have a pleasure boat. Come in today to learn how we can help you.'

On the first day of business a descendant of Johnny Robber himself – a man named Shane Shifty (the family had changed its name after struggling with the stigma of being a Robber) – comes in and asks for a loan. The bank asks him if he has a job or any money. He explains that he doesn't and they assure him that this is not a problem. They are sure that by the time his first big payments come due he will have found a means of paying, and if not, the pleasure boat will be worth more then than it is now and he can simply sell it to someone else and pay off the loan and the interest in one go. It's a win win situation. Shane needn't put down a deposit, and for the first two years all he must do is pay five Vims a month. He's sure that he can find work as a house painter to make these payments. They're sure he can too. He signs on the dotted line and gets his Pleasure Boat Loan. He goes to Priskly Priscilla's Pleasure Boat Shop and buys himself a big Pink Pleasure Boat. In honor of his distant ancestor, and as a statement on his family's reclaimed pride, he calls the boat, Robber's.

He rides it up and down the big lake near the bench he lives on. His friend Martin Crack asks him one evening over a beer where he got the money to buy a pleasure boat. He tells him and the next day Crack heads over to Sharpe Prick's Bank and secures himself a similar loan. The new business is good for the pleasure boat sellers. They don't make the pleasure boats themselves of course, but import them from Crimson Land. The Valleyian boat sellers spray-paint them and offer the service of writing a name of the buyer's choice on the side. The easy loans keep business booming and soon new boat shops start opening up. As an added service, Sharpe Prick's Bank, offers 'Make-em-up' loans, in which they loan money to customers who want to kit their boats out with sound systems or granite top tables. In fact, as Sharpe-Prick's Bank points out, it's not really a loan at all. They call it 'equity'. They determine the value of the pleasure boat and then allow you to, 'turn your boat into a personal ATM.' This means that you have the ability to draw out from the bank a percentage of the value of your boat: pre-approved! Why not use the equity in your boat to help you decorate your boat? It's frighteningly obvious. This idea is enormously popular and as a consequence there is a boost in business for those Valleyians who import either granite tables or sound systems from Crimson Land.

Very soon everyone in the park where Shane Shifty lives owns a pleasure boat. Shane makes money working once a week at the poodle parlor and on Saturdays he takes an old lady's cat for a walk. He manages to make the five Vim monthly payment and the manager at Sharpe Prick's bank is impressed by him and asks why he doesn't use his pleasure boat – which is now an asset – as collateral for taking out another loan. With that loan he can buy another pleasure boat and rent it out or kit it up (with a loan that they will give him) drive it every other day, and then sell it on for a profit. Shane likes the sound of this and secures a new loan and gets a new pleasure boat, which he kits out with pink leather seats, a state of the art sound system, a big screen television on the deck and one underneath the boat to, as he says, 'keep the fishes entertained'.

His friend, not to be outdone, also gets a loan for another pleasure boat and kits it out with five plasma screens and a special sound system that can play music underwater to, as he puts it, 'make the fishes boogie.'

Soon Shane has five pleasure boats. He's used each one as collateral for the next, and he has managed to rent one out to foreigners for a week over the Christmas holiday. The money he makes from that week is enough to pay the monthly payments on all his boats for three months.

The Valley is booming and Banksy's press is too hot to touch!

But that's just the start. With the success of Sharpe and Prick's business plan many such banks begin to open up. Sharpe and Prick, financial innovators of note, have also come up with another excellent idea and they've got their friends on Banksy Street to buy into it. What they do is take all the loans from Shane Shifty and his friends and write them up on a piece of paper. Then they give that piece of paper to their friends on Banksy Street. The guys on Banksy Street, also financial innovators, get these pieces of paper from all the banks and staple them together. Then they take these stapled collections to their friends who work at Alan's and Alan's. They are able to see that, although some of these people will not be able to pay back their loans, the fact that there are so many of them, means that the chance that all of them will not be able to pay back their loans is infinitely low. Thus, they encourage the bankers to put as many loans as possible into the stapled packages, as this will spread the risk about. Sharpe and Prick continue to source their customers carefully and ask Shane and his friends to please bring in as many of their other friends as they possibly can. In the interim, the guys who work at the banks have got the stapled groupings approved as AAA investments and are selling them off to pension funds and other private investors in the Valley and around the world. The beauty of these packaged loans is that they can themselves be used as collateral for taking out another loan. Financial innovation is in a golden age, and it's soon possible to take out a loan to buy the loan packages and then use them as collateral against a loan you may need to take out.

Because the bankers on Banksy Street are recognized as the world's greatest financial innovators, as masters of finance, people across the world are happy to pay for all the products they make. The paper dribbles across the world and everyone owns a bit of it. The idea is that over the years, those who own these special products – which they name derivatives – will receive a guaranteed stream of income when all the guys who took the loans start to pay them back. At first it may just seem like a trickle, but Sharpe and Prick have worked a clause into the loan contract that ensures that after the first two years the amount of money the borrowers need to pay back will double. By then everyone is confident that the borrowers will have found ways to double their incomes, and if not, the value of their pleasure boats will have increased so dramatically that they'll be able to sell them off to someone else and use that money to cover the loan and all the interest.

A lot of investors like these products so much that they ask the banks if they can buy them and leverage themselves up. In order to do this the banks on Banksy Street create funds made up of collections of the loans which they then leverage up at ratios of 3:1 or 30:1 or 100:1. This means that for every Vim the investor puts down, he is able to 'control' or 'own' 100 Vims worth of the product. In order for the banks to do this, they need to secure loans from one another, and in order for there to be enough money to ensure these easy loans, Banksy must do his bit and keep printing. And he does.

In order to counterbalance the potential dangers of being highly leveraged the innovators on Banksy Street develop funds that short sell the products they have packaged together using the loans from Sharpe Prick's. These funds can also be leveraged highly.

Of course this means that the value of the funds made up of the derivatives goes up, and the share prices of the banks that give the loans go up. Everybody is winning.

But one day some investor notices that the stream of income is not what it was supposed to be. He is a builder who lives in the land of the Cheesemakers and he had swapped a large dairy farm for these pieces of paper that guaranteed him income for the next twenty five years. He asks the bankers on Banksy Street if they would mind telling him where the money is. The bankers explain that they are not directly responsible for the pleasure boat loans but that they will be happy to help him out and ask the bankers at Sharpe Prick's where the money is. They do this and the manager at Sharpe Prick explains that Shane Shifty has changed his name to Johnny Robber and left the country. What about his friend, they ask him. He died of an overdose they say. And what about their other friends. They're all bankrupt. And their friends? Dead. And their friends? Broke. And their friends? Bankrupt. Dead. Broke. Left the country. Died. Gone. Changed address. Changed name. Not here. Unfortunately it turns out that everyone in the Southern Part of the Valley who bought a pleasure boat or – as was often the case, several pleasure boats – cannot pay back the loans. The two year grace period has passed and although they were convinced that all the millions of people they gave loans to would use their grace period to find constructive ways to pay them back, they were – they are terribly sorry to say – wrong. Now everyone in the Valley is trying to sell his or her pleasure boat or pleasure boats at the same time, and hence the resale price of pleasure boats has gone down. But didn't Banksy himself appear on television recently and explain that the price of pleasure boats could never go down? He may have, the banker admits, but unfortunately he too was wrong. Everyone was wrong, and they're very very sorry.

—⁕ XVIII ⁕—

THE FALLOUT AND THE AFTERMATH

In which the problem is obvious but no one cares.

The Sharpe-Prick derivatives (SPDs), as they became known, were so popular in their heyday that every bank and every investment firm on Banksy Street has bought them and recorded them on their balance sheets. When the derivatives were seen as a great investment, bankers didn't know or care how many the other banks had bought. But now that Shane Shifty and his friends are unable to pay back their loans, and the Sharpe-Prick derivative scheme is revealing itself to be a farce, there is a massive breakdown in mutual trust.

To keep in line with the central bank's rules all banks have to have at least ten percent of the money they've lent out, on hand. They're always relying on one another, borrowing money to meet these requirements. It's common practice for bankers to call up other bankers and secure instant loans to meet their holdings requirements. But suddenly things are getting tricky. The standard question bankers are asking each other is, 'how many SPDs have you got?'

The same bankers who in the preceding years had been delighted to stock-pile SPDs, and were known to sing their praises at banker parties, now swear they've never heard of them. Although it was not officially made public, almost all bankers are aware of the Lyst brothers' infamous Lying Banker Calculations (LBCs). A banker's LBC score indicates the probability of his lying in any verbal interaction. The brothers calculated that the average banker scores 93 percent. But since the fallout, the calculations show that this average has risen to 115 percent. One investment firm even puts together a product that offers investors leveraged exposure to this rising average.

The bankers all know that the other bankers are up to their eyelids in SPDs, and that if they lend out any money it will certainly end up being used to cover the borrower's losses. So no one will lend and no one can borrow. Because of the sudden restrictions on credit, they are also scared to lend to anyone else. No business can get credit. No one can access any money. The financial systems of the Valley, and soon the whole world, come to a grinding halt. They call it the Debt Induced Doldrums (DID).

At the same time the firms on Banksy Street that have been making and peddling SPDs, begin to fall apart. A famous investment firm, Black Panther Holdings, is the first to go under. It appears that almost half of its revenue was coming from SPDs. With all the pleasure boat loans going bad at the same time, their revenue stream dries up overnight. They have no money and no one will lend them anything. A few days later they declare themselves bankrupt.

The financial systems of the Valley, and indeed those of the entire world, are deeply interconnected and the collapse of Black Panther sends shockwaves through them. Many other banks and companies around the world have accounts with Black Panther and rely on it for funding on a daily basis. With the fall of the Panther, these businesses, dependent on fast and easy access to credit, also collapse. It looks as if the entire financial system is going to implode and Banksy and Rich meet with the heads of all the biggest investment and retail banks. They sit the bankers down and ask them to try and be honest. They understand that this has been proven a mathematical impossibility, but they need them to try!

'Try to estimate just how many SPDs you have on your books', Banksy says. 'And what do you estimate the fallout effect will be if you go under because of your bad SPD investments?'

A famous Banksy Street Banker, Samuel P. Basket from the legendary family, asks Rich to please leave the room. He says that they will be talking about very complex mathematical things and they don't want him asking too many questions and slowing things down. Rich can barely stand he is so insulted, but Banksy assures him that he will keep things in order.

The next day Rich is invited back and they present the plan to him. It's called Banking Industry to Government Transfer of High Equity Fund Tradeoff: BIGTHEFT.

'Have we learnt nothing from our past mistakes?' Rich asks, and slams his hand on the table.

'What mistakes would those be sir?' Basket asks him.

'Leaders before us have implemented plans in which the problem was described in the acronym. This mistake is blatantly obvious. It's written here in black and white.'

'This is no mistake sir. You need to take tax payers' money and use it to bail us out.'

'But that's plain theft.'

'Well, big theft, to be precise.'

'But how am I ever going to sell this idea to the people?'

'You're the politician sir. We're merely bankers' says Basket, before walking away to join Banksy who all the while has been staring out of the window into the darkness.

This is the midnight of Rich's career. He cannot believe what he's about to do, but by the morning he's come up with a way to sell the idea to the people.

Some generations back the Valleyians committed a massacre and almost completely wiped out a group of people who lived in the northern part of the Valley. They were known as the Theftian People, and although the massacre itself was never directly addressed, it has become an accepted part of Valleyian culture to pay 'tribute' to them, by, for example, naming sports teams after them, or selling fancy dress costumes that look similar to the clothes they used to wear. Rich decides to cash in on this trend and tells the Valleyians that one of the Theftians great leaders was a chief known as BIG THEFT. He was a hero, and this heroic operation is named in his honor.

When the journalists start asking questions he pulls a Bob Note and disappears off stage leaving his aide to handle them.

Backstage the shenanigans continue.

Basket explains that Rich must issue hundreds of billions of new government bonds, and raise the money, either by borrowing from the Crimsons or private lenders. If and when that is not enough, Banksy must crank up the printing press and use the money he makes to give loans to Rich. Rich must use all this new money and – in accordance with the BIGTHEFT proclamation – take the money he has from his tax collection, and give it to the big investment banks to stop them from collapsing. He must also guarantee that more taxpayers money will be available in the future if and when it's needed. He assures Rich and Banksy that no one understands the financial markets like he does, and that no matter what the cost in Vims, it will be better than the alternative. Basket explains that what the government will in effect be doing is swapping cash for equity. With Banksy on their side, they can get as many Vims as they need, and with these Vims buy up large stakes in the ailing firms. This will give the firms the money they need to stabilize and get back to business as usual, and it will also be an investment on the part of the government. Rich tries to raise some objections but Basket simply raises his hand and says, 'not now Rich. Good work on the Chief BIG THEFT thing by the way.'

Banksy fires up the printing press, and Rich opens up his coffers.

Their plan appears to be successful. With the massive injection of liquidity into the banks, and with a guarantee of more support from Banksy if needs be, the bankers start to feel more at ease about lending to one another. Businesses are able to access credit again. But unfortunately the damage has already been extraordinary, and citizens of the Valley have been terribly spooked by the incident. On the news every evening commentators and announcers talk about the biggest stock market losses in decades. They show images of factories being shuttered up all around the world. The DID made a massive dent in domestic spending and this meant a decrease in imports from Crimson Land. Millions of Crimsons are out of work and are forced to leave the urban areas and head back to their village homes. Citizens in the Valley are not as eager to spend money – and are especially anxious about taking on more debt – in the face of this crisis. The decrease in spending means shops like those that sell shirts with bananas on the pockets lose customers and some are forced to close up. As is always the case, bad economic conditions beget bad economic conditions. Less spending means fewer jobs and fewer jobs means less spending.

Then things get even trickier. Banksy has been appearing on television every evening and assures the world that things are under control and that civilization will not come to an end. But what he hasn't told anyone is that he's been getting secret requests from banks in foreign countries for help. Because his bank has for decades been the de-facto central bank of the world, banks in other Vician countries that have been infected with SPDs are asking if he will extend his largesse to them too. They are also on the verge of going under and since the financial products that have almost killed them originated in Banksy's country, they feel that it is his duty to throw them a lifeline, just like he's done to the domestic banks. He consults with some of the local bankers and they agree that the banking system of the world is so inter-connected that if they leave those foreign banks that bought SPDs to sink without assistance, they will risk undoing all the good work they've already done. Banksy, not wanting to see that happen, agrees to fire up his press again and makes interest free loans to numerous foreign banks.

Mainstream economists – or as they are sometimes known – Northern Valley School Theorists (NVSTs), feel that under the circumstances Rich's government and Banksy did admirably well. A prominent NVST advocate, Paul Stoned, is on record as saying, 'There can be no doubt that Chief BIG THEFT would be proud of us all. In fact, I'd go so far as to say he's smiling down on us right now – hang on, do Theftians go to heaven?'

After a few months the big investment firms on Banksy Street are thriving again, and, thanks in large part to the success of operation BIGTHEFT, many of their employees are again able to get large bonuses. With these bonuses they are able to buy many luxury items – some are even known to buy pleasure boats – and this increase in domestic consumption is very good for the Valley companies that import things from Crimson Land, and the shops that store the Crimson goods on their shelves. It also means that some of the new Vims issued by Banksy are able to flow out of the Valley again as they had been doing in the preceding decades. This helps reignite some Crimson industries that had stagnated during the DID.

But there are others, particularly those who subscribe to The Cheesemaker School of Economic Theory (CSET), who are not happy with the way in which the government has handled it. Followers of Csetian theory are strict free-marketeers and they believe that governments must not interfere in the market. They believe that if companies have made bad choices they must go bankrupt. Some say that their theories are harsh and unforgiving, but they believe that if companies and banks understand that governments will bail them out when they make mistakes, they are more likely to act recklessly. Furthermore, they think that free-markets cannot be controlled or manipulated in the long run. If companies have gone bankrupt and are bailed out now, if the monetary base is increased in an attempt to bring about stability, it may appear to work in the short term, but it is in fact only delaying inevitable problems. And when the problems come further down the road they will be even worse. They believe that by bailing out banks and investment firms and taking failed companies and turning them into public institutions, the governments are simply shifting responsibility for large-scale mess-ups from private hands to public hands. In other words, they are punishing the wrong people. They believe that Banksy's money printing operations will, further down the line, cause serious inflation or even hyperinflation.

But for now it appears that the storm has passed. Whatever methods they may have employed, Rich and Banksy have prevented economic armageddon (EA).

PART TWO

⟿ I ⟾

THE STATE OF THE WORLD

Four years after the bursting of the the Great Pleasure Boat Bubble.

The Valley

Four years have passed since The Great Pleasure Boat Bubble (GPBB) burst, and the economy is in the midst of what the government calls a 'delicate recovery process' and much of the rest of the world is calling, 'perpetual decline.' Economic conditions in the Valley are the worst they've been since the end of the Mighty Mighty War. NVSTs believe that Banksy did an excellent job in steering the economy through treacherous waters into relative calm. Without his expert hand, they say, the Valley would have gone into a deep depression and dragged the world down with it. Amongst enthusiasts he is officially recognized as the man who prevented EA. Others – Csetians in particular – feel that the bank's role in the crisis was misguided. They believe that if Banksy's central bank sets a precedent for rescuing reckless institutions, it encourages reckless behavior.

Rich XIII, who recently took over from his father is a charismatic leader and although he inherits a broken economy his charm and public speaking ability brings a wave of hope through the Valley. His policies however are rather vague. Nothing gets better, but things don't get worse either. Despite harsh criticism Banksy keeps interest rates at near zero. Officially he's hoping to get people borrowing and starting up and or expanding businesses. But bankers are still terrified of lending to anyone, so all they do is get interest free loans from Banksy and use them to buy Rich's bonds that yield around three percent per annum for a ten year bond. Critics call it 'free money'. But Banksy ignores his critics. Secretly he's hoping that by keeping interest rates unnaturally low he will spark fears of long-term inflation and thereby get people to spend in the present. If he can do that things have to get better, they just have to! If they don't spend now, he fears a deepening recession and deflation.

In this regard, his policies in fact do work and Valleyian consumers continue to borrow and spend. But as many of his critics point out, nearly seventy percent of the economy is accounted for by domestic consumption. This means that most of the money goes toward purchasing goods made in Crimson Land, and thus the famous outflow of Vims and inflow of goods continues. Banksy also carries on buying up Rich's government bonds, and Rich and his government use the money to try and stimulate the stagnant economy and bring it back to life. Once again, these policies earn both praise and criticism. The NVSTs believe that in times of economic stagnation and depression governments should run deficits if necessary and spend on stimulus projects. Recessions are brought about by a loss of the 'deep lusts' that drive human enterprise, and if there are idle people and unused capital, an injection of money can get things ticking again. Once the 'deep lusts' come back to life, the economy will boom and the government will be able to pay off the deficits. Economic revival comes from spending not saving. The Csetians believe that economies can only recover when there is genuine demand for economic goods and services. Government interference cannot change reality, and economies will only heal naturally with time when bad companies have gone bankrupt and debts have been settled. Running deficits only creates bigger problems down the line.

The Valley, however, still has many things going for it. It allows for intellectual debate and freedom of expression. It has the most widely recognized and idealized popular culture. It has a positive birthrate and allows for immigration. It has vast tracts of land and natural resources, and is still the world leader in many fields. It has by far the world's largest army, and the Vim is still the world's de facto reserve currency. But the Valley is not recovering from the recession, and talk of deep and lasting depression is rife. Many Valleyians, and people all around the world, are convinced that the sun is finally setting on the Valley.

The Island

To many the Island serves as an ominous warning to the Valley. Although the territory itself is infinitely smaller, the population is about one third the size, and the economy even at it's peak was less than one third that of the Valley's, it was and remains a major financial power. But the Island's Big Bubble (Buburu as it's known locally) – a bubble in stocks and real estate – burst eighteen years before the Valley's. It was in large part caused by the Valley during the days when Bob Note was the head of the central bank. His easy money policies led investment banks to borrow heavily in order to speculate, and at this time the Island seemed like the most attractive prospect. The Islanders themselves were very well off by world standards, and had lots of extra money. They got caught up in a frenzy of property and stock buying, and their money and that of the Valleyians and even the Cheesemakers, helped inflate one of histories greatest bubbles. As is always the case during bubble season, reason was the first victim. No matter where the bubble occurs or what sector it's in, those caught up in it tend to believe that reality has finally been overcome, and growth will go on forever and prices will never come down. In the case of the Island, the people have long held a belief that they are uniquely unique. This belief is shared by many people around the world, and so both those inside and outside the Island came to believe that their unique and mysterious ways, meant that the bubble economy was not a bubble at all, but a new paradigm with new possibilities. When it burst, many ordinary Islanders had second and third homes repossessed, lost their life savings on the stock market, lost pensions and life time employment jobs. This led to what the Islanders and others called, 'the lost decade' which led into a second 'lost decade' when the economic recovery never came. The stock market still sits at eighty percent below its high.

But the term 'lost decade' or 'decades' is in many ways misleading. The Islanders continue to enjoy one of the highest standards of living in the world, and their excellent medical facilities have meant that average life spans have continued to increase during this period. Unemployment is extremely low and there is almost no crime. There has been deflation and prices and wages have gone down or remained the same for over twenty years. One of the reasons that the country was able to continue plodding along despite the massive collapse was that Islanders were and remain extremely diligent savers: especially in comparison with Valleyians. During the boom years Islanders on average saved thirty percent of their earnings. This has meant that Island Banks have vast deposits. Measured in Vims the savings add up to trillions. Banks have kept their interest rates at zero for over twenty years and there is almost no legitimate borrowing by businesses looking to start up or expand. They only have one investment option: government bonds yielding one percent per year over ten years, which, in a deflationary environment actually equates to two percent real yield. This has given the government enormous breathing room as they have been able to issue infinite bonds, borrowing constantly from their banks, and hence their own citizens. They have essentially been following the NVSTs ideas: running deficits and trying to stimulate growth. They have built countless airports, roads that run in concentric circles and others that lead to nowhere. They have built thousands of bridges, joining small islands with two inhabitants to other islands with one, to other islands with none. All of this spending has left the government with a debt of 240 percent of its gross domestic product, and although it has kept unemployment under control it has not reinvigorated the economy at all.

The Island has always had a very strict work ethic, and during the years of fast growth they worked long hours. Since the bubble burst, however, there is much less work to be done. But appearances are very important and it's simply unthinkable that people should go home early or take vacations. Instead there are millions of 'zombie workers', who only have an hour or two of legitimate work to complete in a day, but spend ten or twelve extra hours in between pretending to work. They tap on keyboards, take books down from shelves and put them back up again. They stare intently at their computer screens and copy rows of numbers from pieces of paper onto electronic documents and back onto paper. They pour numerous cups of coffee, wander up and down the corridors at high speed, have long conversations with each other and have meetings about meetings and keep records about records. Every office, company, school, university and organization of any kind has countless workers in their 'admin departments'. The Islanders fill out thousands of documents and love using stamps. It is socially acceptable to fall asleep at one's workstation. In the old days this was a sign of being overworked. Today it's a sign of life-threatening boredom. But no one knows how to address the problem or what to say, and so instead they continue reminding one another that they are the hardest working people on earth.

The Island's problems are further compounded by the fact that they have the largest aging population in the world, a negative birthrate and a pathological addiction to the national pension. In the post Mighty Mighty War days there were eleven workers for every retiree, but today that number has decreased to two. One of the mottos on the Island is, 'You must have a pension!' And that does not mean private pension, it means state pension. And so state pension funds have invested massively in government debt and helped keep the public works spending spree going.

During the boom years the Island developed and advanced some of the world's most widely used technologies. It became one of the greatest manufacturing and engineering countries, and many of these famous companies continue to produce and export goods to the world. But as happened with the Valley, many of the factories have been exported to Crimson Land where wages are lower. But the trend was not as extreme, and during the two lost decades the Island managed to steadily record trade surpluses. This meant that they were able to pay for the import of raw materials and oil with this money. Maintaining this positive trade balance is of vital importance for the Island, as it has no natural resources. And in its latest economic report, the Islanders posted a trade deficit. Many believe that this is the start of a bigger trend.

The Cheesemakers

After the Mighty Mighty War, the Cheesemakers and some of the surrounding countries started a very slow and laborious process of partial integration: a process that in the past decade has intensified and subsequently led to problems. The Valley too was once made up by various smaller states joining together in union. But their union was held together by common laws, tax systems, and a shared language and culture. But this is not the case with the countries that have joined together in the union with the Cheesemakers. They don't much like each other and tend to have negative stereotypes about the other countries. All the same, in the past decade the union has adopted a common currency. When the union formed they chose the name Dairy Union Monetary but Not Fiscal Union Congress System. Under the advice of a well-known former Literal but converted Ironic acronymologist – Dr. Joe Shortandtight – they decided to omit the word 'Not' when forming the acronym, giving them the name DUMFUCS. Critics believe that this omission is the reason why those involved did not realize that the problem with the Dairy Union Monetary but Not Fiscal Union Congress System was that it was a monetary but not a fiscal union congress system. They all shared the same currency but were still free to determine their own tax codes, retirement ages, pension plans, set their own budgets and write their own laws. In other words each country was free to independently influence many of the factors that determine a currency's strength or weakness.

But there was an even bigger issue with the monetary union. In the past, countries with smaller economies and less widely used currencies, would only have been able to borrow in major foreign currencies and only to a limit and at a rate determined by the bond market. Weaker countries' currencies would also have been correspondingly weaker, and thus have made their exports more attractive. But this new system has dealt a double blow to the weaker economies. Firstly, having the same currency as the Cheesemakers – a strong one – hammered their exports. Secondly, the bond market knew that because the smaller countries were borrowing in the currency of the Cheesemakers their debt was effectively backed by the mighty Cheesemaker nation. This meant that they were able to borrow large sums of money at extremely low interest rates. And borrow they did. The weak countries thus found themselves in a position not entirely dissimilar to that of the Valley during the post PWOS-NOM-FOR days: they had a currency that was stronger than their productive output would usually have allowed. And this meant that they were able to finance a higher standard of living than their productive output would otherwise have allowed. During the early years of the Daiso – The DUMFUCS currency – everyone was a winner. On their own the Cheesemakers would have had one of the strongest currencies in the world, and so the system enabled them to keep their currency weaker and their exports more attractive. The fact that their poorer neighbors were able to borrow more, meant that they spent more: often on goods imported from the Cheesemakers. All this led to several years of serious boom. But eventually reality caught up with DUMFUCS when the bond market called timeout on the borrowing habits of the small country, Homerstandt. They had borrowed far more than they could possibly pay back and lenders started getting nervous. To take on the extra risk they wanted more reward: bigger yields on the bonds. And so the interest rates are going up. And just as it happened all that time ago in the Valley, a death spiral begins. Higher interest rates mean more of the budget must be spent on interest payments, which means more borrowing, which means higher interest rates. It's not good. Homerstandt has borrowed vast sums of money and the people live well beyond their means. People take long paid holidays and after several years of work are allowed to retire on a state pension. Those that do work, dodge tax, and many years ago most of the ambitious people left Homerstandt for other countries to set up corner cafes and sell gold necklaces. The country's economy is in fact rather small, but the problems it's suffering from, threaten to spread to other, large DUMFUCS nations if the Cheesemakers are not able to contain this crisis.

Most people would probably not have heard about it, but news networks like Wolf and PNQ have taken an active interest in it and have reporters, 'on the scene' to keep Valleyians and others up to speed with the events as they unfold. Many commentators believe that this is actually a conscious tactic on their part to help divert attention away from the Valley whose finances are actually in a worse state than the DUMFUCS

The Cheesemakers have given Homerstandt several emergency bailout packages on condition that they make massive spending cuts, and impose austerity measures. These measures have led to large-scale job losses and pay cuts. These cuts have hurt the average Homerstandtian badly and there are protests in the streets and buildings are set on fire. Lenders have also been hit hard, taking 'haircuts' on their original investments. Bonds due for immediate maturity have been converted into longer term bonds, payable for example in ten years time as opposed to six months. But despite all these measures everyone is basically in agreement that Homerstandt is going down. The Cheesemakers are doing everything in their power to keep things afloat while the other DUMFUCS nations have time to insulate and prepare themselves for the imminent collapse of Homerstandt. Other big borrowing countries are imposing austerity measures at home, and the big banks are cutting lending and trying to build up large reserves of cash to protect themselves. It is well known that most DUMFUCS banks have lent money to Homerstandt and the other teetering nations. The Cheesemakers and their central bankers have to assure the private banks that Daisos will be available if the situation calls for it. Although they are afraid of inflation, they will fire up the print if needs be. This is certainly preferable to a breakdown of confidence amongst banks as happened during the DID days. As is to be expected Csetians insist that Homerstandt should just go bankrupt ASAP. They think that keeping bankrupt countries artificially solvent causes bigger problems than letting them go under. They believe the lenders were reckless and should pay the full price for their bad decisions. But politicians and bankers don't tend to agree with this view. And they'll do what they can to prevent a crisis. And if they can't prevent it, they'll postpone it and have it another day.

❖

The Crimsons

The general belief is that the Valley is declining and the Crimsons are rising. There's good reason to believe this. The Crimsons have the world's largest population and have become the largest manufacturing nation. Their economy has grown enormously, raising hundreds of millions of Crimsons out of poverty. Their middle class is constantly expanding and their GDP grows by ten percent each year. They've recently overtaken the Island as the world's number two economy: something that the Islanders – who generally consider the Crimsons to be inferior, backward and noisy – have found very difficult to swallow.

They have for decades been posting enormous trade surpluses and have built up massive reserves of foreign currency. They continue to pull off large-scale smoke and mirror operations to keep their currency undervalued and pegged at a set rate to the Vim. The fact that they have massive surpluses of cash just when the rest of the world is struggling gives them an extraordinary advantage. Their representatives travel the world with a large checkbook, signing deals with anyone, anywhere, who can help them secure their future needs. They are also increasingly seen as the international lender of last resort: the go-to guys when the going gets tough. Their deep pockets have turned them into the Valley's personal banker and it's estimated that they hold over a trillion Vims worth of Valleyian Government bonds. There is constant talk of Valleyian default and people speculate about what the Crimsons would do if their investment were destroyed. Most believe that the Valleyians will not default on their debt out and out, but rather keep the printing press going and inflate their way out of it: paying back their debts in massively devalued Vims. Almost everyone makes a big deal out of this. Of course the Crimsons don't want to see an investment in excess of a trillion dollars destroyed. And of course the interest they get from it is nice. But with an economy growing at the speed theirs is, a few million in interest payments lost isn't going to break the bank. What really matters is respect, power and status. When that's been lost it's harder to recover. The Crimsons don't want to be seen as a country that lets debtors get away with behaving badly. So, even though their Valley investments are anything but guaranteed they keep buying up bonds (though in increasingly smaller amounts) and begin suggesting that they may help out the DUMFUCS if push comes to shove. They want to expand their influence as far as possible, and have thus far shown a preference for using soft over hard power. Though they are a growing military force and already the banker to the world, they are sensitive about international perception. They've been known to cave in on certain issues under international pressure. Many liberal leaning commentators consider the Crimson government guilty of major human rights abuses. These are regularly dragged up at meetings between themselves and the Valleyians.

Despite their aura of unlimited power and their projection as a nation capable of sustaining eternal growth, the Crimsons have many troubles of their own. They have been growing faster than any other nation in history, and in the process have caused environmental and societal chaos. There is a huge gap between rich and poor. For decades the Crimsons had a one-child policy and many parents would get rid of their daughters in favor of sons. This ingenious policy means that there is a generation with too many men and not enough women. The women of course love it. They're able to pick and choose. The men on the other hand are forced to either be top quality, high earning, good-looking, well-spoken, smooth, sophisticated heartthrobs, or lonely masturbators. Cities filled with sexually deprived deviants will inevitably lead to problems. Crimson local governments have also borrowed vast sums of money to finance massive development programs and these loans are understood to be implicitly backed by the central government, leading some to say that the Crimsons are facing a debt crisis of their own. They recovered from the fallout of the GPBB at a speed that left the rest of the world slack-jawed. It turns out however that the Crimson government also went on a printing spree to keep things ticking along smoothly, this money has ended up fueling a construction bubble that some fear could have more catastrophic effects than the GPBB when it bursts. Recently they recorded a trade deficit. This had been thought all but impossible in the preceding decades. They have made their money importing raw material, adding value through cheap labor and then exporting. But a growing middle class means rising labor costs, and more domestic consumption. Things will inevitably start shifting from here on out.

There are still however hundreds of millions of citizens who have not yet achieved middle-class status, but aspire to it, and economically speaking their potential for growth appears limitless. Many enormous challenges lie ahead for the Crimsons. But if they are able to overcome them, they will most likely live up to their designated role in the standard narrative of the day and become the greatest power on earth.

─◦ II ◦─
THE DUMFUCS

Where it is better to FUCU than be a DUMFUC.

Animosity is rising between Homerstandt and the Cheesemakers. It represents a general rift that has developed. The Homerstandt and the other Southern DUMFUC Zone states, or as they are now more commonly know, Homerstandt Associated Group States – HAGS – have been accused of many things by their smug northern neighbors: laziness, lackadaisicalness, languorousness and an array of other 'l' words. These kinds of generalizations don't help matters. But other than a few agitators in each state, everyone in the DUMFUC Zone knows that for better or worse this marriage has been consummated. There's a lot of theatrics and grandstanding for domestic political purposes, but there's no going back now.

With the second bailout negotiated and completed, the private bondholders are taking bigger haircuts. The markets and the media have turned their attention away from Homerstandt for the moment. They have reduced Homerstandt's Debt to GDP ratio to a projected 120 percent in ten years. The DUMFUCS have bought more time. Soon after this the DUMFUCS central bank injects massive amounts of liquidity into regional banks. It basically gives them interest free loans over 3 years and the DUMFUC banks lap up the debt like pigs at the trough. But they have a plan. First order of business is a name change, for they have come to realize that a monetary union that is not also a fiscal union is not such a great idea. Also they realize that DUMFUCS rhymes with 'Dump trucks' and they worry that some people might have poked fun at this name. The new name they come up with is the Fiscal Union of Cheesemakers United – FUCU. This doesn't sound at all like 'Dump trucks' and member states are satisfied and unanimously vote in favour of this new acronym. To go with the new name they also implement tougher fiscal rules for FUCU Zone members. These rules to prevent overspending by FUCU Zone governments probably don't go far enough to form a true fiscal union. But the truth is that most FUCU states probably couldn't stomach a true fiscal union like that of the Valley's anyway. This puts the long-term future of the FUCU Zone and their currency the Daiso in doubt, but in the medium term the changes should help a great deal in keeping their houses in order. But in order to survive the FUCU zone must become more competitive, and that's going to be the tricky bit. It is generally agreed that all the FUCU countries – not just the HAGS – must cut minimum wages, thin out government sectors and public sector wages, and become more efficient. The Cheesemakers new motto is 'Government jobs are only for losers'. They encourage the best and brightest to go into private industry. They even put a maximum test score on public sector job aptitude tests. Only the most mediocre are good enough. They encourage school students to only continue as long as they need to. Here they introduce another motto 'Don't waste your life at school – drop out and into an apprenticeship'.

On the sidelines another deal is taking place. For centuries some of the eastern states in the FUCU bloc have had disputes with a nation known as the Carpetmakers. The Carpetmakers not only make carpets, but also have lots of oil. They are hated by most FUCU people and also by the Valleyians and their government. It is suspected that the Carpetmaker government is manufacturing a Very Big And Awful Bomb (VBAAB). Rich fears that the VBAAB will be aimed at the Valley, and so he and his government set up private meetings with some of the Eastern FUCU States (E-FUCUs). They negotiate a missile base to be set up along their borders. Should the Carpetmakers try and launch a bomb, the integrated defense shield will fire the missiles automatically and take it down. The base will be known as Strategic Hotspot On Open Terrain (SHOOT). The Valley will pay the E-FUCU states a set monthly rate for hosting SHOOT. The offer comes at a time when no FUCU state can say no to money. Banksy promises Rich that he will print him all the money he needs. Because the Valley will be paying for the privilege of the base, they will not have any other obligations to the host countries. It is thus referred to as a 'non-treaty'. The operation is officially known as the SHOOT Alliance Mutual Agreement Non-Treaty – SHOOTAMAN. Agents from both the Classical and Literal Acronym Schools complain about this name. They insist that it is misleading, as SHOOTAMAN has no intention of actually shooting a man. The Ironical School believes that the name neither shows up an inherent problem nor states the obvious, and is hence a failed acronym. But all three agents are assassinated by an E-FUCU ex-secret serviceman and buried in the holes dug as foundations for SHOOT

On the main stage another nine months pass and as predicted the next episode of the Homerstandt Sovereign debt crisis is upon them. It is worth mentioning here the difference between a Sovereign debt crisis and a run-of-the-mill bond crisis. In a Sovereign debt crisis the state borrows in a different currency. This time for Homerstandt it is more like a Sovereign debt crisis because even though it is their own currency they don't hold the keys to the printing press. The FUCU does. And the FUCU controls the monetary policy. In a way this is good – a blessing in disguise. They must face their problems head on and solve them before they become so insurmountable that they bring down the whole system.

The FUCUs are prepared. They have created firewalls around Homerstandt and have a plan. They have analyzed Homerstandt's economic assets to determine what has the greatest potential for generating a consistent income stream for creditors. Homerstandt's economy is dominated by several key sectors: fruit markets, corner cafés, gold chain manufacturers, gold chain sellers, gold chain marketers, gold chain repairers, gold chain insurers, and tourism. During the crisis many gold chain insurance companies have gone bankrupt, as many gold chains were lost or destroyed in the riots. This has given a temporary boost to the other gold chain related industries, but the sector is not strong enough to satisfy creditors. Fruit is looking good, and corner cafés are always en vogue, but everyone knows that the shining jewels in Homerstandt's tin crown are the world famous islands. It is thus agreed that creditors will receive equity in the form of a constant income stream from the many Homerstandt Island Resorts (HIRs). A fund is created – the financial powers like to create 'funds'. It goes without saying that the fund will be given an acronym. It is called the

Homerstandt Island Procurement (HIP) Fund. Some in the Ironical School believe that using the acronyms HIP and HIR sounds too comical considering that the powers are not trying to make a comic statement. But the Cheesemaker leadership threatens them with legal action and they shut up.

On the finance front it is decided that the bondholders will swap all their long maturing bonds for a 30 percent stake in the HIP fund. The Homerstandt government will receive a 40 percent stake in this fund and private investors will be able to take up a 30 percent stake. Islands will be promoted to investors and potential customers worldwide. One large island will be targeted specifically at Crimson investors. All the facilities will be directed at satisfying Crimson holidaymakers' needs. All decorations will be strong, bright, deep red – because Crimsons consider this color to be auspicious. This will be a type of exclusive economic zone where companies won't pay tax. Demand for a share in this fund is astronomical, particularly from Crimson and FUCU countries. The lease of the islands to the HIP fund will be for 30 years. After which time the Homerstandt government will have the option of extending the lease or dissolving the fund and divesting the assets.

Homerstandt's debt is reduced to 120 percent of GDP in current terms and contagion – a technical term used by investors and smug people to describe a complete loss of faith in government – has been averted. With this precedent set, investors and creditors know that should the worst happen and a FUCU Zone country default, they will not receive worthless longer maturing bonds but something with real physical value that the government has a stake in – be it a soccer stadium, wine producing area or equity in a media company. The harsh austerity measures implemented over the past three years have ensured that Homerstandt products and services are becoming more globally competitive and the size of the government has shrunk. During the austerity days – ADs as they became known – the Homerstandt government raised the age of retirement from 28 to 40. They tried to make it 50, but the Homerstandtians kept burning things until they brought it back down to 40. The next year they register mild economic growth, and again win the coveted International Gold Chain Maker's Award (IGCMA). During the riots they lost out to another HAGS nation. With the rioting now over, many Homerstandtians take up soccer hooliganism and this gives a boost to the private medical industry.

The other HAGS are not home free and many structural problems exist, but one strong point within the FUCU Zone is freedom of movement. A mobile workforce enables residents of HAGS to move out if they really want to. If the price of labor drops too much in a FUCU Zone country, capital will move in and invariably reinvigorate it. This takes time to restore balance but in the end balance is restored.

Cheesemakers increase their domestic consumption and start driving their own homemade luxury cars and using their own precision-engineered products. Some of them even decide to take holidays to HIP resorts for a few days a year. The age of retirement is raised to 90, and the average life expectancy increases to 76. They now boast the highest paying pension scheme in the world, with the average retiree getting the equivalent of 10 times the annual income per month. This small but extremely wealthy group of nonagenarians create a niche market for savvy investors. Gold-plated Zimmer frames and diamond studded colostomy bags prove popular amongst these smug oldies. Some of the highest paid jobs in the FUCU zone are for private nurses.

One problem for the FUCU zone states from this point onward is their strong currency. The Daiso strengthens rapidly after the FUCU Zone crisis is resolved and this hits exporters hard. Luckily they realize that a strong currency is good for a country or states that have a balanced, well-structured economy, and so the central bankers don't attempt to devalue it. The people gain purchasing power and imports of raw materials become cheaper. Without excessive government intervention and bailouts, some companies will thrive, others will fail and new companies will spring up to replace them. This is the natural, inescapable order of a free market. This free market will undoubtedly benefit some and hurt others, but the FUCU states seem comfortable with this. The future for the Homerstandtians and the FUCU people in general looks bright.

· ⌒ III ⌒

THE ISLAND

Where the biggest catastrophe is the change in thinking.

The 'Very Big Dam Catastrophe' and the resultant 'Disastrous Aftermath Madness Nuisance' – DAMN, have dealt a knockout blow to the Island. It was the biggest hydro-electric dam in the world and when it broke, it killed thousands of residents and wiped out the main industrial areas that had been deliberately based close to the cheap energy source. Some say it is ironic that the potential energy stored in the massive dam that had powered the economy for the last 60 years has been its ultimate demise. The world was shocked at the scenes of destruction televised in real time. Cities were flattened and it reminded many elderly of post war Island. With time these industries can all be rebuilt, and though devastated and scared, the survivors eventually get on with their lives. But the change in perception remains – hydropower is not safe. And this is a lasting blow to a country where more than 70 percent of energy needs come from hydro power. The Islanders no longer want this cheap environmentally-friendly power source. They can never again trust the companies that run them. Prior to the disaster a massive public-works project had been underway to fix the aging hydro-electric infrastructure. But now 90 percent of the power-stations are mothballed – too old to be safely run again – and new stations under construction are halted. Thermal power stations are fired up again and the shortfall is made up from conscientious citizens and companies chipping in to save their share of power. The scramble is on to source as much natural gas, and coal as possible. No one is willing to be the first to put themselves out there and say it, but eventually a foreign correspondent living on the Island writes, 'This is a Damn Catastrophe.'

The Island has been fighting an overvalued currency now for at least three years. It relies heavily on exports to drive economic growth, maintain near-full employment, and sustain their relatively high standard of living. A year after The Very Big Dam Catastrophe – almost to the day – the central government finally succeeds in weakening the Isle. Not, however, through their now tried and tested method of selling their currency on the market. After peaking at 75 Isles to the Vim, the ICB (Island Central Bank) drops a bombshell. For the first time in memory it will set an inflation target – at 1 percent. Most people didn't even notice when, a week before, the head central banker, Chipin Chopu, was called into the prime minister's office for a 'very important meeting'.

No one knows exactly what happened behind the closed doors, but it is believed that the aging Prime Minister, Kannot Do, sat him down and explained that these were special circumstances. He promised Chopu that they would find other buyers, that a tax hike was coming soon and that this was the only time he would ever ask. Chopu most likely understood that these were not requests, but instructions, and that if he didn't do as Kannot Do asked, Kannot Do would find someone who would.

The next day Chopu announces that there will be a massive round of bond buying. It was time to fire up the Island designed, Crimson manufactured computer again, for some more mouse clicking money creation.

The effect is sudden and catches many observers by surprise – 80 Isles to the Vim, then 85 and 90 as speculators cover their short Vim positions.

A few decades earlier, Island housewives – who control the family purse strings (and some say their husband's lives) – came up with a nifty 'Island Style' plan. Local Island banks had not been offering them real interest rate returns and they were fed up. They discovered however that in countries like Bruce Kingdom or the Land of the Wild Animal they could get massive returns on their savings. And so something known as the 'cross it over trade' – CIOT – was born. Economists around the world marveled at the shrewdness of these housewives who with absolutely no financial training were able to make more money than they were. With improvements in technology these housewives were soon able to do the trading themselves from home. International markets started referring to these women as Mrs. Handova – a common Island surname. As Islanders' savings have always been enormous, the apocryphal Mrs. Handova has been a force to watch – and imitate – ever since. Her decisions sway world markets and especially effect currencies. As the Isle begins to lose value, Mrs. Handova realizes that now is the time to cash out her family's remaining Isle denominated savings. The Isle begins to flee the country and The Bruce Kingdom Vim and Land of the Wild Animal Round start to gain.

The government has finally gotten its wish and broken the back of the stubborn Isle. As many at the time say, 'this will surely help exports.' But few – not even the internationally renowned Mrs. Handova – could possibly have guessed what was to come.

Mr. Kannot Do and his government continue with their shenanigans. They've been talking about it for a while now, and the time for implementation has come. The tax hike is meant to shore-up the central government's fiscal books. Officially, it is 'to help us all become a better and more prosperous Island.' Unofficially, Kannot Do and his team know that they're stealing their citizens' money – at least that which Mrs. Handova hasn't gotten out of the country – to buy themselves more time. They've convinced the citizenship of the need to raise the consumption tax to 10 percent. As is usual in the Island, it is not hard to convince the people when urgent action is required for the sake of the country. They are a very compliant people and responsive to authority figures. Once the members of authority are convinced of the change needed the general public very quickly fall in line. The tax is introduced over 3 years in two parts – first to 7 percent and then to 10 percent.

Until now, even with a declining economy, the Islanders had still been able to maintain a high standard of living. Essential needs such as designer handbags, cell-phone covers, shoes, necklaces, bracelets, jewelry and little 'cutey cutey oh so cutey' fluffy things, were still within the reach of most middle class households. The main reason for this was deflation. Every day, every year, every decade, their massive savings were slowly gaining in purchasing power. All an Islander need do was take his box of cash and bury it in the ground and it could buy more the next year when he dug it up. Some say this is why Islanders saved too much. In reality, saving was a long tradition and deflationary prices just exacerbated this tendency.

The tax increases provide little fiscal support for the central government, but have massive consequences for the entire country. Domestic consumption dries up. From young families who were already struggling, to pensioners who were eating into their life savings, everyone slows their spending. So instead of having more money the government now has less. It hits companies too, and the Island enters into another recession.

On average an Island Prime Minister's term of office is somewhere between 3 and 4 weeks. Somehow Kannot Do has managed to stick around for a couple of years. But people are getting tired of him, and in usual Island fashion, he steps down. He is replaced by Kandobut Dont, a man who at first shows a lot of promise.

At first the lack of spending stokes even more price deflation, but this deflationary era is coming to an end. Teenagers and those in their twenties have never seen it, but old timers know it well. They remember clearly how when they were young, shortly after the Mighty Mighty War, they were paid 3000 Isles a month. During the boom years wages increased to a peak of 600,000 Isles per month. When prices rose in tandem with wages these old timers were able to live well, borrowing money and paying it off quickly in slightly inflated Isles. The Island grew steadily and everyone was happy. But this time there's a horrible twist. Prices go up but wages don't.

As the Isle continues to weaken toward the psychological 100 to 1 against the Vim level, the unintended consequences of the Island government's actions become apparent. For a number of years, due to worldwide money printing, commodity costs – food, energy, metals – have all been rising. This had been substantially offset by the strengthening Isle. The media forgot to mention this and instead regurgitated meaningless phrases and showed pictures of 'cutey cutey so cutey' things. For 20 years employees had been accustomed to taking pay cuts or at the very least not asking for increases. The word 'Iesu' was even lost from the Island language and they had to import the Valleyian word 'raise' when they needed a word to express the desire for a higher wage. Because of this culture and the remaining poor economic conditions, price inflation, especially in imported food and materials far outstrips wage inflation. The Island is entering into a phase of the dreaded stagflation. But this is just the beginning, or what some commentators call, ACT 1.

Following the development of stagflation, and gradually increasing interest rates, the central government's fiscal position continues to weaken. The current account deficits that first appeared a few years ago are now the norm. Because of the weak Isle and the country's new dependence on foreign natural gas and coal, national energy costs have skyrocketed. Foreign policy becomes increasingly dominated by energy security. This deflects criticism away from internal folly. 'Peace-keeping' missions gradually increase in scope and number, and the nation changes its pacifist constitution to allow the export of military technology – to allies of course. This stokes regional competition – especially with the emerging power, the Crimsons. The ultimate consequence of this is the Isle government's continued reliance on deficit spending. This culminates in ACT 2 – the Island bond crisis.

Foreign investors had finally deserted the Island after realizing the true state of affairs. It was not a 'safe-haven' after all – more like a Bermuda Triangle. They'd watched their capital depreciate because of constant money printing.

As Csetian economists have always warned, once you start going down that path there is no turning back. Bigger and bigger stimulus is needed to achieve smaller and smaller gains. According to Csetian theory once money printing begins, the only possible outcome is fiat money returning to its use value: burning paper; and, some say, toilet paper. But according to those who've tried it, this is in fact inaccurate. Money does not work well for wiping.

Luckily for the Islanders they still have a lot going for them. They love their currency the Isle, and so a complete loss of faith in their money is delayed, if not ultimately prevented. It has already lost much of its purchasing power and now it takes 130 Isles to buy 1 Vim. But the government assures them through the usual channels of authority that it is all under control and that the rot has stopped. One benefit is that slowly but surely the Island becomes more competitive again and exports start picking up.

'If only energy costs would stabilize and the Isle would strengthen a little' many say. Overseas vacations are only for the super rich now – those who are involved in procuring energy for the Island. As with all bond crises, a banking crisis is right around the corner. Isle banks have been hiding losses for years, but they're not able to hide anymore as they bleed to death from their government bond losses. The central bank has to provide liquidity to keep them afloat. They all had plans to get out of bonds at the right time but that right time never came. As the value of Government debt starts to decline the government puts pressure on the holders to keep the debt on their books, offering super cheap loans and easy money. The tipping point is finally reached when the government is forced to admit that the debt is unsustainable. The Debt to GDP rings in at a massive 300 percent. In the end it was of no importance whether the debt was internal or external. If anything the fact that it was internal, only bought them more time, and this time they used to dig themselves into an even deeper hole.

As the crisis deepens we begin to notice something very interesting happening on the Island. Farmland has been idle for decades and rice fields are overgrown and unrecognizable. The average age for farmers is 98. Anyone under 95 is referred to as, 'young man' or 'young woman' and is expected to do all the heavy work. In the preceding decades it has not been commercially viable to go into farming, and the young generations have left their family farm lands and headed for the cities. But as the crisis unfolds many begin returning to their grandparent's and great grandparent's land. Record post MM War unemployment and rising food costs are starting to make it economical and even profitable to return to farming, and once almost-abandoned villages, start coming back to life.

Back in the cities things are not so pretty. Even though tough austerity measures and public selloffs have stabilized deficit spending, the stagflationary depression continues. A new word spontaneously emerges on the Island to express this idea – 'stagu-depu-re'. The interest rates push through the 4 percent barrier – the point after which most governments are unable to manage, and wherefrom, statistically, there is little chance of a turnaround – and fast approach 6 percent. This level is unsustainable and the central government is running out of buyers. A global forum is held and the big players, The VIC Trio plus the Crimsons – VIT+C come up with a stabilization package. They will create a fund to buy Island government debt to support the government's austerity program and try to hold interest rates below 5 percent to prevent a full blown banking crisis. Most commentators, however, agree that this fund is not big enough to provide long-term support. The ICB also offers internal banks massive loans at lower interest rates to increase liquidity and prop up their balance sheets. This combined with more bond buying from the ICB, stabilizes things for the moment, but the Islanders' situation is becoming critical. Official inflation is running at 10 percent p.a. and unemployment has risen to 12 percent, which for this proud and work-loving people is almost unbearable. At a rate of 10 percent inflation with no wage increases, people can't afford fuel and have to increasingly use public transport. But even this becomes unaffordable as local governments have privatized much of the local transport system. The companies that now run them struggle to pay for fuel with an Isle that trades at 150 to 1 against the Vim. They are forced to raise prices or risk bankruptcy themselves. The Islanders still maintain their trademark manners, and ticket sellers will say, 'we are very sorry to charge you this price. It is not our will.' It becomes a set phrase and soon everyone in the Island is using it. The standard response is, 'we understand it is not your will and accept your apology.' The exchange is followed by a bow. As the Islanders have short distances to travel, bicycles are frequently used. Men who used to drive cars but have switched to bicycles are called, 'downgrade bike man' or 'downubiku'. Scooters were already popular but now the roads sound like beehives, as the Islanders dart about, their helmets glistening in the sun.

Since the end of the MM War the Islanders have developed a pathological obsession with the national pension. For the past seventy odd years citizens, or companies paying on their employees' behalf, have made regular contributions to the government run fund. This fund invested mostly in government bonds – for safety. But the easy money of the past has kept their yields relatively low. Now that the Island population is graying and redemptions of pensions have been increasing, the pension fund has become a net seller of government bonds. This has put added pressure on the Island public debt market and the government now puts a stop to this. The Government passes legislation increasing the age of redemption to 70. It can't reduce payments because of the ongoing inflation but maintains them at pre-inflation levels, in effect eating away at retirees' income. The legislation also includes a clause to oblige the central bank to purchase these bonds as they are sold. This guarantees liquidity and ongoing pensions. The Csetians call it 'just more money creation.'

The time for the final act has come.

The crisis re-emerges quicker than anyone would have imagined. Despite the best efforts of the global community there are not enough funds to hold down the Island interest rates and they begin to soar. First to 10 percent and then to 15 percent. Banks collapse under the weight of their massive losses on government debt and inflation climbs to 30 percent and then 40 percent. It's during this time that we witness the most extraordinary social changes.

The Islanders have always been recognized more as 'perfecters' than innovators – they import a foreign technology and improve upon it. During the time of high inflation some industrious Islanders come across the Inflation Machines used by the Valleyians in the days when Bob Note was head of the central bank. The Islanders now put their famous technical skills to work and convert these clunky old hand-turned devices into electronic masterpieces. They call them Digital Inflation Machines (DIM). Restaurants, shops, clothing stores, drug stores, even the few remaining pet stores, use these devices. They are connected directly to the central bank and retail banks, and collect information from gas importers. They attempt to measure the market price of gold, oil and Vims and through a complex set of equations set price increases (at the predicted market price) for products. Prices are recorded on large digital boards, and with numbers constantly rolling over, supermarkets look like airports or stock exchanges. A famous Island columnist says, 'this just goes to show that even in inflationary times we are unique.'

But then electricity becomes too expensive and these boards are taken down or unplugged. Mrs. Handova luckily has a lot of her money saved in foreign currency, and she is able to import her savings back in and keep ahead of the ghastly inflation. But not all housewives were as smart as Mrs. Handova, and many Islanders now rush to get rid of their Isles and swap them for anything they can actually hold – most especially of course, they want and need rice. Thus, those Islanders who had seen the writing on the wall and moved back to their ancestral lands before the serious inflation began are sitting more than pretty. Islanders are forced to hand over vast quantities of Isles for bags of rice, and soon – as is to be expected – Isles are no longer accepted by the farmers. They want physical things. The Islanders hand over beautiful dresses, brand name handbags, decorative ornaments, and millions of the 'cutey cutey oh so cutey' little fluffy things they'd collected in the good days. During this period of awful inflation – some even suggest it should be classified as hyperinflation – the farmers' wives and daughters become the 'cutest cutest girls' on the Island. They are able to show off all their 'cutey cutey oh so cutey' things, and inspire envy and hatred amongst their peers. The city girls cannot bear to see their country cousins looking better than them. They call these girls, 'country cuties', a derogatory term.

Rice cannot easily be bought in shops any more, and must be acquired in the countryside through bargaining. City dwellers have converted rooms in their houses for storing the large quantities of rice they've acquired. And very soon we begin to notice that rice is actually being used as money. Shops start accepting rice in lieu of worthless Isle notes, and again, because the Islanders are natural technological innovators, 'Rice Vending Machines' RVMs start popping up. They store cool drinks, alcohol, cigarettes – all the things the old coin machines used to offer – but now they accept only rice as payment. You pour your rice into a large chute in the front of the machine, and it quickly and accurately weighs it and blows it into a small silo behind the machine. Then, out pops your product, and if you've overpaid, your change – in Isle coins.

The RVMs are effective, but also drive home the ridiculousness of the whole situation, and within a month of their release Kandobut Dont steps down as PM. He is replaced by Justdo Pleasu.

The government admits that its bonds are worthless and puts a moratorium on bond redemption and interest (coupon) payments. A massive reorganization now begins and the banks that remain solvent are given debt for equity swaps. They are handed the keys to the high-speed rail systems, ferry services, publicly owned tobacco companies and freeways. They will retain the rights to earnings on these key pieces of infrastructure for 50 years. The government will issue a new currency. The New Isle is pegged to the Daiso at 400 to 1. The ICB believes that the Daiso will fare better over the long run than the Vim. As soon as the new currency is released, inflation starts to come under control, and the barter style economy vanishes.

New bonds are issued in this newly pegged currency. The New Isle bond issue, coupled with the equity swap leaves the Debt to GDP ratio at 100. This now is a sustainable level and confidence is regained in the Island. It is still a number of years before private institutions are completely confident to lend to the Island government again but stability seems to have returned. Inflation plummets, and slowly the lives of the Island people begin to return to normal. One big upshot of this crisis is that, with the Isle dramatically devalued, the Island is able to export cheaply. Its factories start to re-open and employment picks up. The Island seems to have a more balanced economy now. Farmland is being more productively used – farmers' daughters are still referred to as 'country cuties' – and manufacturing is directed better at both the needs of the domestic consumer and export market. The very inefficient service sector has been thinned out and people now seem more capable of doing things for themselves. There is now no need to have a man from the electronic super-mall come around to your house to plug in a new toaster. When the Islanders go to work now they actually do work and don't just pretend to work. They are more driven and upbeat about the future and even begin to get married and have little ones again. Sons and daughters leave home when they are young adults and go out into the wide world like they did generations before. The Island has a promising future.

—๑ IV ๑—

THE CRIMSONS

With an economy that's on fire.

The average Crimson is less concerned with the rising of their country's status than they are with the rising cost of living. The Crimsons are suffering from serious inflation: the kind of inflation that would have made Bob Note's hair stand on end. The inflation started the same way inflation always starts: the central bank issued too much money. After the GPBB central bankers around the world injected trillions of Vims worth of liquidity into their banking systems to try and combat DID and get people borrowing and spending. As the Crimsons were the ones manufacturing most of the elements needed to drive the GPBB, when the bubble burst they were particularly hard hit and the Crimson government followed their impulse and hit the print button. But their currency, the Crimo – unlike the Daiso, the Vim and the Isle – is not convertible outside of their country. This means that they are not able to share their inflation with the rest of the world. All the currency remains trapped within the borders, making, as a famous local economist put it, 'one big rumble!'

Inflation is in double figures, and though the Crimson government does their best to blur these facts, the man on the street knows the truth. Some salaries are able to keep up and others are not. Banks have been unable to offer savers equivalent returns. They are highly regulated and their reserve ratio requirements can be changed at the drop of a hat. The stock market has done very well over the long run, but remains highly volatile (massive individual losses are commonplace) and Crimsons – many of whom are first generation wealth holders – become increasingly reluctant to put their hard earned money at risk. And so the only option for the Crimsons is real estate. Everybody in the world knows that real estate is the best way to protect your wealth. After all, house prices – like pleasure boat bubble prices – can only go up. And so the Crimsons have been investing in real estate at astronomical levels. There have been literally millions of apartment blocks built in Crimson cities and it's not uncommon for an up and coming Crimson to own two or three apartments. But prices have been going up for years, and it's obvious that there's a major bubble.

There are however some important differences between the Valley's GPBB and the Crimson's current housing bubble. The main difference is credit and creditworthiness. As we saw, the Valley's bubble was born when Rich's government proclaimed that every citizen was 'entitled' to a pleasure boat. Sharpe Prick's and similar banks made loans available to people who had no money and no jobs. The Crimsons however are slightly stricter when it comes to offering loans. If a Crimson wants to buy a first property they must put down at least forty percent up front. If they want a second it goes up to fifty and if they want a third they have to pay the full amount. This makes it impossible for the Crimson equivalent of Johnny Robber (whose name happens to be Sing Sang Shoot) to acquire a condominium for himself, let alone another few for investment purposes. And this means that as the bubble begins to deflate, the consequences will not be as severe. Unlike in the Valleyian housing market (and pleasure boat market) banks won't be left with millions of homes or boats that were bought on speculation by penniless buyers. There is also nothing equivalent to SPDs, and so the fallout will not have the same knock-on effects.

But the Crimsons are not immune to stupidity. They have a hierarchical system of government and local leaders need to meet certain minimum growth targets and report back to the Capital. If they fail, the local leaders will set them on fire. The fastest and most reliable way for them to meet their growth targets is to build big things. When the central bank issued trillions of Crimos, the local councils – who are not allowed to borrow directly – set up numerous fronting companies and borrowed through them on a massive scale. The central government of course is completely aware that this is going on, and encourages the banks to lend to the local government proxies instead of independent borrowers. The local government officers, in their formal capacity, stood surety for the loans they'd taken out through their proxies. The central government in turn stood surety for the local divisions. With this borrowed money they went on a building spree unlike anything the world had ever seen. Of course they'd been building before, but with manufacturing work slowing down after the GPBB, the construction boom absorbed many unemployed workers. They've built impressive towns with enormous shopping malls and high-rise apartment blocks. They've built entire cities with massive museums and impressive archways and awe-inspiring multi-lane roadways. In Crimson Land they are very fond of calling the things they build 'of the people' – The Great Museum of the People, The Great Hall of the People, The Great Lake of the People. This tendency now has some sadly ironic consequences, as the new cities 'Of the People' have everything to make them truly great cities, except people. Everyone is convinced that the people will move in soon enough but for the meantime the common folk cannot afford to pay for the expensive new apartments, and so though most have been bought as investment homes by rich Crimsons, they stand empty.

In other areas of Crimson Land the local governments have built, New Up Towns (NUTs). They have constructed enormous shopping centers (often comparable in both size and design to their ancient buildings), on the outskirts of town. The Crimsons are, and always have been, very fond of drawing attention to their own greatness. Their modern buildings (much like their ancient ones) have grandiose names like the Grand Mighty Fantastic Mall of the People. But unfortunately many of the grand mighty shops have yet to find tenants.

The Crimson government is doing its best to try and deflate the bubble they helped cause. They've been raising interest rates constantly and have raised banks' reserve requirements numerous times. As with local government leaders, bankers who fail are set on fire. Some outsiders believe that this method is cruel, but most Crimsons are convinced that the government is their big brother and best friend and the protector of Crimson culture. Burnings are thus more widely accepted than in other countries. The Crimsons claim that during the time of the GPBB Banksy kept interest rates at near zero right up until the day the bubble burst, thereby keeping the party going on for way longer than it otherwise would have. They say that by raising their interest rates and increasing reserve requirements, they can deflate it slowly and prevent a major fallout. They are right to some extent, but are unable to avoid a 'hard landing'.

At the same time that interest rates are rising and credit drying up, the value of property across Crimson Land – especially on the east coast – begins to fall. As most investors are first timers in the property game they are taken by surprise. Property sellers start going bankrupt and some are set on fire by buyers who were guaranteed that their investment could only increase in value. The government responds by setting the fire starters on fire. With the value of their investment homes falling, many first generation wealthy Crimsons start feeling poorer than they did, and so spend less. The Crimson government and much of the rest of the world had been hoping for a boost in domestic spending and this slump is a massive disappointment. With the slowdown in construction millions of workers are laid off and many return to their ancestral villages. Others remain in the cities, and find new ways to make money. Luckily most Crimsons are excellent hustlers and very astute at identifying business opportunities. Their booming tourism industry (both locals and foreigners like to travel around the country) offers many opportunities. Some Crimsons become artists, others rickshaw drivers, others tour operators or sellers of tee-shirts, plastic goods, statues, shoes, rings, guidebooks and teapots. They undergo hypnotic sessions after which whenever someone says, 'no thank you', they hear, 'please ask me the same question again right now'. This is very effective, as they never lose hope in closing a deal. They offer 'special prices' to everyone, and through their tenacity are able to earn a living and feed their families. But the slowdown in construction still has a major knock-on effect through the economy. Local mining companies are hit badly, as are importers of raw materials. Bruce Kingdom, a country that had been heavily reliant on exporting commodities to the Crimsons has its first recession in decades. In fact many commentators begin to proclaim the end of Crimson Land.

They had been growing at a rate of between 9 and 10 percent per year for the past few decades and this rate at first slows down to just over 6 percent. Then – though the numbers remain in such controversy that no one ever knows the truth for sure – it is understood that the growth rate ultimately slows to somewhere between 3 and 0 percent for a full two quarters. This was completely unthinkable just a few years before and it gives much of the world a serious fright. But the negative growth rate doesn't last long, and the recession ends quickly. Crimson land, however, does not get back up to its 9 or 10 percent annual growth, and settles somewhere between 5 and 6 percent. Although this is still higher than almost all other countries in the world, even this rebound is not enough to keep creating jobs at the rate Crimsons are urbanizing. It is likened by a prominent commentator, Ying Cringcrong, to a multi-car-pileup. Millions of citizens keep pouring into the cities, but the system that absorbs them has stopped moving. Moreover the government is still trying to contain the fallout affects of their previous stimulus project – inflation and mal-investment – and so they're not too keen to fire up the printing press just yet. Despite the recession, prices in the cities remain, for many, unbearably high and social unrest is rife.

Problems are further compounded by the collapse of the 'shadowy banking system' (as it is informal it has no acronym). Although the Crimson leaders do everything in their power to control borrowing, they are ultimately unable to exert absolute authority over people's lives, or alter human behavior. When Crimsons are unable to borrow from the banks they turn to one another. Friends borrow from friends, nephews from uncles, sons from fathers, desperate borrowers from loan sharks. And these are not small loans. They add up to trillions of Crimos and are responsible for funding a frighteningly high percentage of overall economic activity. When money cannot be sourced within Crimson land, they turn to their friends and family on a nearby island called Crimo Bong. The risks of course are large, and the borrowing costs correspondingly high. And when recessions come and borrowers are unable to pay back debt, there is no legal recourse for lenders, and so they follow the Rule of the Fire. It states: *Be you Brother, Friend, Nephew or Son, pay me money or fire will come.* Borrowers who cannot pay back their debt are, in accordance with the law, set on fire. It is of course illegal to borrow on the black market, but for the most part the government doesn't know who's doing it. If someone has a grudge against a borrower however they can squeal and get the government to kill the borrower, by setting them on fire. Many, afraid of their creditors and the government, jump off roofs, throw themselves into fast flowing streams, blow their heads off with borrowed guns, or in some cases save the lenders or government the trouble and set themselves on fire. It's a messy, messy business.

But things are not all bad for the Crimsons. In the preceding decades the middle-class has swelled massively and the older generation invests obsessively in their children's education. This policy is starting to pay major dividends, as increasingly large numbers of young Crimsons are highly skilled and educated. More technical and advanced industries begin to grow and compete internationally. When housing prices were peaking young adults could not afford to move out of their homes even after graduating from university. It is a Crimson tradition for middle-class parents to put down the deposit on their children's first home (provided they're a male and have found a wife). But during the time of high property prices this became impossible for most families (and many men and women would live at home well into their thirties). As the prices come down however, normal middle class families and young married couples are able to enter the property market again. New couples set up homes and need to furnish their apartments. Many of the goods they need are produced locally and so this gives local producers the boost they need. Empty apartments fill up and new ones are built. Some of the ghost towns come to life. Also, because Crimson Land is massively unregulated (in terms of labor) compared with the Valley or the newly formed FUCU, it is very easy for businesses to start up again quickly. Workers who lost their construction jobs (and didn't become successful hustlers) often find themselves employed in factories again. During the time of easy Crimos and big borrowing there was a lot of mal-investment, but there was also a good deal of intelligent investment and much necessary infrastructure was built. Train lines, roadways, dams and electrical plants continue to help the economy even after the credit has dried up.

The Crimson leaders had established the reputation as being the banker of last resort, but during the years of 'Crimo-Pumping' as it became known, and the subsequent housing, construction and ghost town boom and bust, they found themselves in a less favorable position. Countries with work forces even poorer than their own have started competing as exporting powerhouses, and with the revaluing of the Isle and Island labor prices, they're finding themselves in direct competition with their favorite enemies. This means the government is less happy to lend out money to anyone and everyone. But the fact remains that when the rest of the world went into a deep recession, the Crimsons – by hook or by crook – managed to avoid one, and so had lots of money when everyone else was bankrupt. They were able to negotiate from a position of strength and secured energy and commodity deals that they look set to benefit from for a long time to come.

With time the Crimson government has learnt a number of tough lessons. Most importantly, as an exporting nation whenever one of its big buyers goes down, it feels the pain: right in its groin. To get themselves out of these gluts, they can 'Crimo-Pump' and risk inflation and mal-investment; but in the long run the only way to insulate themselves is to ensure that their economy shifts towards domestic consumption. Analysts (Not the Alan Lysts but a local Crimson group called, Ichecku) explain that if Crimson workers fear they have no safety nets they will save obsessively. This means that the government needs to regulate industry more and help make workers feel more secure. If they feel secure, they're more likely to spend. Reluctantly, the government starts spending more on social security. It ceases to lend money to the Valleyians, and can be less relied upon to bail other governments out. The increased regulations make it more difficult for anyone to start up a business on a whim, but the sense of security it brings to workers and middle-class alike, means they do begin to save slightly less and spend slightly more, and so the Crimsons become increasingly less vulnerable to the shocks of the outside world. The growing middle class however, also means that they are not the 'export only' country they once were, and regularly have months in which they record trade deficits. This was, a few years back, almost as unthinkable as the Valleyians recording a trade surplus.

Social conditions continue to improve in Crimson Land. The Crimson are fond of saying, 'always getting better, bit by bit.' A well-known Crimson Sociologist, Mr. I. Watch, develops something known as the spit-o-meter (SOM). Through a set of ingenious equations he shows how the decrease in Crimson spitting corresponds to an improvement of social conditions. Three decades ago, Crimsons would spit anywhere: on trains, planes, boats, inside restaurants, at work, in their offices, even at home. Today, there is no spitting inside restaurants or on public transport and almost no Crimson spits at home. Spitting on the street however is still commonplace, but I. Watch predicts that within the next decade spitting will be confined to modern spittoons. He even predicts a boom in the spittoon production business. In the decade after that he foresees private spit bags that will be used only in desperate situations, out of sight of other people. Thereafter, spitting will vanish all together and by the end of the century there will not even be a word to describe spit or the act of spitting. As the incidence of spitting has decreased, so have the number of crimes punishable by burning under Crimson Law. Two decades ago 27 894 different crimes could lead to execution. Many were very trivial and obscure. They included crimes like late returns of videos, giving a dog a name inappropriate to its gender, leaving ice to melt on a wooden table and stopping to tie one's shoelaces on the street. Today there are only 14 992 crimes that carry the death penalty, and I. Watch predicts that by the time spitting has ceased the death penalty will have vanished. Social ills such as murder and theft are – in perfect alignment with his complex SOM-calculations – also on the decrease.

Like the Islanders, the Crimsons have a large aging population, and as on the Island (and most of the rest of the world) women live longer than men. The Crimson's one child policy has led to there being too many young men. A strange social phenomenon thus emerges: men in their late thirties give up on looking for a young wife and instead marry a seventy or eighty year old widow. The Crimsons call this, 'Youngmanhang' which translates from Crimson roughly as, 'pink lip grey nipple.' This seems particularly bizarre to the outside world, but also intriguing, and more and more foreigners come to Crimson Land to experience its 'mysterious' culture. The Crimsons work hard to make themselves more attractive to the rest of the world. They have big bright cities and good universities that help with this goal. Sometimes however their behavior overseas harms their international image. During the DUMFUCS crisis, large semi-state owned corporations bought up chains of islands in Homerstandt. They enforce strict 'Crimson only' policies on their Island and only let local Homerstandtians onto the islands if they dress in ancient Homerstandt style clothing, serve them grapes and perform other, 'Homerstandtetic activities'. The islands become a source of great fascination and intrigue, but no one outside of the Crimson elite and their servants are allowed onto these 'Crimson Red Isles'. The servants never divulge details. They are, after all, the highest paid workers in Homerstandt.

Aside from this, the Crimsons international reputation steadily improves. They make a 'concerted effort' to burn fewer dissidents in public, and make efforts to improve domestic social conditions. Their culture of investing heavily in education means that they increasingly lead the world in scientific development. This irks the Valley no end. They also spend more and more on their military. Small countries wanting to snuggle up to the Crimsons, offer themselves up as land-bases. The Crimsons thus start setting up international bases across the world, making the Valleyians, who issue a statement that says, 'That's our job!' extremely nervous. In terms of military spending however, they remain in second place.

But eventually their economy does overtake the Valley's and becomes the world's largest. On that day the Crimsons have a big celebration and sing many songs in honor of Big Boss 'Kitty Cat' Meow, whom they still revere as a hero. An unofficial anthem called, *The Biggest Cat*, is written by a famous songwriter who happens to be the wife of the Big Big Leader (BBL). The leadership spend three months practicing this song in anticipation of their debut on the day the Crimson GDP officially surpasses the Valley's. They meet in the Vast Impressive Extraordinary Wonderful Amazing Hall Of The People (VIEW-A-HOT-P) and the ceremony is broadcast across Crimson Land. The BBL and his wife stand on stage together and sing. The party members (PMs) respond with the set refrain, Meow Meow.

The song begins.

The cat has wagged its tail
Meow Meow
He's eaten all the fish
Meow Meow
He's the biggest cat in the whole wide world, and he's eaten all the fish.
Meow Meow.
The cat was born in an alley
Meow Meow
He lived off scraps and bones
Meow Meow

And so the song continues. Written in traditional Crimson style, it has three hundred verses in which the BBL and his wife describe the cat's rise from lowly beginnings, to its current status as 'the cat that ate all the fish' – a reference to a well loved ancient Crimson parable. At the end of the ceremony, a three hundred meter wide, five hundred meter long, four hundred meter high cat shaped helium balloon is released into the sky. As it passes over the Vodka Drinkers' country it gets shot down.

They condemn this action and the following day release another, even bigger cat, that luckily blows in the opposite direction.

The whole world, except for the Island, now recognizes the Crimsons as having the largest economy in the world. The Islanders have recently started a program called Restore National Pride (RNP). It was in large part started in response to the Crimsons continued rise to power. As part of the program they instituted something called New Improved Economic Measurement (NIEM). They have a unique way of measuring the Crimsons' GDP. They do not count exports or construction and so rank the Crimson economy as the tenth largest in the world, one place behind their own. NIEM is always subject to change, and should the Island economy drop another place, it will ensure that the Crimsons do too. Some NIEM workers have suggested that in the future they may stop counting domestic consumption and agriculture as part of Crimson GDP.

With the slow inward adjustment of their economy their standards of living and average income have continued to rise. Their economy settled into a kind of boom and bust cycle not entirely different to the Valley's, though their finance laws remain stricter and their central bank tends to act sooner when trying to stop bubbles. But years of keeping their currency all at home have finally proved far too costly. When the economy slows down seriously they struggle to import commodities, and this leads to lagging recessions. Inflation has become so entrenched in their lives that many forget there was ever a time when it didn't exist. They finally let their currency become fully convertible, but because of years of backlog vast quantities of it flow onto the market and it loses value, forcing their economy into another shock downturn. The Crimsons and much of the world are surprised, and in a panic reflex they consider taking it back off the market again. But they don't, and after an initial downturn it begins to value upwards against the Vim and Daiso settling at around 3 to 1 and 2 to 1 respectively. When it settles at 1 to 200 against the Isle it triggers a spate of 'honor suicides' on the Island, but the NIEM workers use tried and tested smoke and mirror calculations to bring the Isle back towards the culturally acceptable 150 level. Foreign exchange counters unfortunately do not accept these calculations and so many Island travelers under-budget for their Crimson Land vacations, and are met with a nasty shock on arrival.

The Crimo does not take the Vim's place overnight as the world's reserve currency and never rises to a position comparable to that held by the Vim at the height of its power. But the world slowly shifts away from the Vim towards a collection of currencies, with around forty percent as Crimos, and the other sixty percent made up by Vims, Daisos and other less traded currencies.

The Crimsons enjoy their status as the world's largest economy and their culture becomes increasingly attractive to foreigners. Soon enough a young Crimson man does a pop rendition of *The Biggest Cat* and it becomes a worldwide hit. Teenage girls from the Valley to the land of the Cheesemakers can be heard singing, 'He's the biggest cat in the whole wide world and he's eaten all the fish. Meow Meow.'

— V —

THE VALLEY

In which there's no way to skin a CAT.

By historical levels this so called recovery is very weak. This means that for the foreseeable future there is no possibility of the Valley increasing its tax revenue, and thus if Rich does not make serious spending cuts, he has no choice but to continue borrowing. But borrowing is not difficult for Rich. Traditionally his government's bonds have been considered the single safest investment in the world. Furthermore the Vim remains the world's reserve currency and Banksy can always quite literally, absolutely guarantee that the lender will get their money back. After all, he can print as many Vims as he wants. But now with many insisting that the Valley is in permanent decline and that Rich's government will never be able to pay its way out of debt, why do locals and foreigners continue to clamber for Valleyian debt? Simply put, they have no choice. There is no other market in the world that can even remotely compare with Valleyian bonds when it comes to liquidity. Billions of Vims worth of bonds exchange hands every day, and so they can get vast amounts of money in and out of the market at high speed. No stock market can withstand that kind of movement and commodities cannot be bought up at that bulk without affecting the price. Only with Valley bonds can you sell a few billion Vims worth in a day without causing a run for the exit, or destroying the value of the remainder of your investment.

But the laws that govern billions are not the same as those that govern trillions. Both the Crimsons and the Island have, respectively, just over and just under a trillion Vims worth of bonds. In recent months there was a big brouhaha made when Rich's government was forced to raise the 'debt ceiling': the amount of money they are legally allowed to borrow. Of course everyone knew that they would in the end raise the limit, but nevertheless this big showdown drew international attention to the fact that Rich and his boys were deep in the hole, and the Alan Lysts downgraded Valley Bonds from their sacred AAA rating. After the downgrade the Crimsons sold off some of their Valley bonds, but soon went back in and bought them up. They even bought up more, and then some more. This started making the Valleyians nervous (they don't want too much debt concentrated in Crimson hands), and the Crimsons said they would slow down in their buying and sold some of their bonds. But many believe that they continue to buy up debt on bulk through secretive subsidiary parties known unofficially as 'Meow Meow Agents' or MMAs. Besides the bonds, the Crimsons also hold another approximately 2 trillion Vim denominated investments, and they rely heavily on the Valley to keep buying up their products. For these reasons some counter the argument that the Crimsons are keeping the Valley's economy alive on life support. They say the current situation somewhat resembles a standoff a few decades back that took place between the Valleyians and a group of bear hunters known as the Vodka Drinkers. The Valleyians and the Vodka Drinkers each had vast numbers of weapons pointed at one another, so many so that if either side fired first and the other retaliated, they would both be wiped off the face of the earth. They called this situation One Shot We All Die No Insanity Please (OSWADNIP). Today if the Crimsons strike first and start selling off their Vim bonds en masse they will destroy the value of their remaining holdings. If they cause the Valley economy to grind to a halt they will lose one of the biggest buyers of their goods and thus send shockwaves through their own economy. As for the Valleyians they could impose the import tax and punish the Crimsons, but then they would force the Crimsons to strike back by selling off their Vim denominated assets, and ceasing to buy Valley bonds.

And so things continue to plod along. Most of the world is caught up with the crisis in the DUMFUCS region, and so pay less attention to the slowly unfolding debt crisis in the Valley than they otherwise would. The economy shows some small signs of recovery and many think that Banksy is a hero, steering the economy in the right direction.

But the Valley's ever-growing debt starts to make investors nervous. There are increasing whispers about insolvency. And the yield begins to shift upwards. This could be bad. It would mean that each year Rich and his boys and girls would have to cough up more just to pay back the interest on their loans. This means more borrowing to meet costs, which in turn means higher interest rates. Many pundits appear on television and exclaim with a mixture of fear and ghoulish exhilaration that the famous Valleyian bond market is about to collapse. And well it might have, had something else not happened first.

The Island crisis begins and the world's attention shifts. Panic and fear grip the international markets and the famous flight to safety begins. Billions of Vims fly across the world into the only place that can accept them. Rich's government stands waiting with open arms and Banksy smiles from ear to ear as the buyers come. The yield drops down to 0.9 percent – just what the Island offered back in its day. At the height of the crisis the Valley offers negative yields for short-term bonds. In other words if you want Banksy to keep your money for six months you'll have to pay him! It's a tiny premium of just 0.01 percent and he easily attracts many buyers. Sellers become buyers and those with major short positions are wiped out. As the Isle collapses the Vim strengthens. The Valley it seems has been let off the hook big time, and the party can go on a little longer. At the height of the bond rally a man named Sylvester Stainbourn, the head of Stainbourn Strategic Services (3S), a hugely successful hedge fund built from the ground up by his father Simon (who was born in poverty), sells everything they own and invests all the money in Valley bonds.

During the last several years it has been discovered that the Valley is sitting on top of extraordinary quantities of natural gas. There have been numerous obstacles to them extracting it on a large scale. Many believe that the extraction process – known as Wack-em-Crack-em – in which high-pressure liquids are used to crack the rocks in which the gas is trapped, is dangerous and damaging to the environment. They call the 'Wack-em-Crack-ems' enemies of the environment. They are in fact right, but this no longer matters. Jobs are jobs and money is money and Rich has given in to the Wack-em-Crack-em companies' demands and allowed large-scale Wack-Cracking to begin. Boom Towns have been shooting up across the Valley and blue collar workers are earning the kind of salaries that bankers were getting in the days of the GPBB. It turns out that the Valley is sitting on enough natural gas to power themselves for the next two hundred years. So much natural gas comes onto the market that it becomes an affordable alternative to increasingly expensive oil. As the Island starts to get itself back into shape, the demand for energy increases and the Valley is looking to position itself as their provider of choice. They use technology that allows them to liquefy the gas and transport it across the ocean. The Island makes necessary adjustments and begins to switch much of its industry onto natural gas. The Crimsons – now the most energy ravenous country in the world – are also hungry for as much liquid natural gas as they can get. But just buying gas is not enough for them. With their large cash surplus and their love of offshore investment they begin to eye some of the larger natural gas startups and instead of buying up more bonds they begin to invest in large-scale Wack-em-Crack-em operations. Their semi-private Valleyian based gas project, Big Boss Meow Meow Crack and Wack (BBMM-CAW) becomes the largest such operation in the world. Having such a long name, most employees choose to refer to it simply as Cat Crack. The Crimsons invest in drilling companies, conversion outfits, and transport companies. They even start investing in train lines and roadways and dam projects. In exchange for their investments they get equity in the projects, and a constant and reliable income stream. Nationalists complain that the Crimsons now own half their Valley. But really, once they get over the 'insult' to their pride, they're able to enjoy all the benefits that come with fully operational Valley-wide infrastructure. Others, of course, don't know who the Crimsons are. Valleyians are very parochial and most can't accurately point out a single other country on the map. Many used to think that Crimson Land was a district in the southern part of the Valley, and were filled with patriotic pride when they saw 'Made in Crimson Land' labels filling up their shelves. A beauty contest winner, when asked what she thought about putting import duties on Crimson products – admittedly an unfair question for a beauty pageant contestant – said, 'what's the big deal? We're all Valleyians aren't we?'

Extreme right wingers – dominated by Ventak fundamentalists – believe that Mr. Tak disapproves of Crimsons coming into the Valley. They claim that this is a crime against Mr. Tak's sacred name, and that he has sworn vengeance if all the Crimsons don't leave. Unfortunately no one is able to confirm or deny this statement, because only Mr. Tak's 'chosen leaders' are able to communicate with him. The Ventak fundamentalists are also staunchly anti-plastic-surgery. They claim that Mr. Tak made everyone in his image and that to distort this image offends him. Even during the Valley's darkest days they are somehow able to win supporters and challenge Rich's power, by being staunch 'anti-plastics'.

Finally the Crimsons let their currency float and become fully convertible. At first it is extremely volatile, but eventually settles at around 3 Crimos to 1 Vim. The stronger Crimo has a negative affect on the Valley's middle-class borrowers. For years banks had been offering very low interest rates. One of the reasons they were able to do this was because the Valley's banking system could tap the savings of the Crimsons. Some called it the Vim cycle. Vims would flow out of the Valley into Crimson Land only to be lent back to the Valleyians at low interest rates. With the Crimo's increase in purchasing power the Crimson middle class have increasingly embraced consumerism and have consequently been saving less. This means that the days of easy credit are a thing of the past for Valleyians. They are forced through programs that are described as 'semi-voluntary' to start saving again. The decrease in Vim purchasing power, and constant inflation, has slowly eroded away their standard of living. But the Valleyian middle class has not disappeared as some once feared, and the Valley has not become a third world country. The weakened Vim has made imports increasingly more expensive, and this has in turn made locally produced products more competitive. Moreover, with their boom in natural gas, the Valley has come close to gaining energy independence. With increased import costs they have been forced to turn all available land into productive farmland. The weakened Vim allows them to export their produce at a competitive price. They have enough food to sustain their domestic market. Some states within the Valley declare themselves business and investor friendly. The BAIF states, as they become known, charge very low taxes to businesses and have fewer regulations. They succeed in attracting back many offshore Vims as well as bringing in plenty of Crimos. They are happy to watch as the Crimsons' currency builds up in their bank vaults. Some call this process 'reverse Vimosis'. With the Vim's power decreasing internationally, the issuing body – Banksy's Central Bank – is not the all-powerful institution it once was. Many local banking outfits have in fact unhitched themselves from the Central Bank and do not hand over their Crimos in exchange for Vims as Banksy would prefer them to. They are increasingly able to use their Crimos to buy goods on the international market, and even within the borders of some of the BAIF states certain businesses accept Crimos. This means that something resembling a dual-money system begins to emerge. In some states there even appears to be a tri-currency system. When fear of hyperinflation was at all time highs, many investors and traders slowly started turning to gold and silver as a protection. Some states began accepting the precious metals in lieu of fiat currency, and this practice remains in place today. There is even talk of a more inclusive commodity money, and a system whereby value is stored and measured in terms of energy.

In short Banksy and his regime have lost a lot of their power. In fact if one looks at the Valley now it is obvious that the biggest change is a shift in power from the bankers to the farmers and the Wack-em-Crack-ems and the industrial workers. Blue-collar types, farmers and those industries that directly support them are making lots of money and SPD peddlers are just getting by. Of course there are many problems. As some had warned, Wack-em-Crack-eming does indeed cause major environmental and ecological damage. The biggest problem is that when things go horribly wrong it poisons water supplies. Thankfully, the Valley has maintained its position as one of the world's leading technological innovators, and water purification systems that can turn poisonous water into drinkable water at extremely low cost are widely available. The Valley exports this technology to the rest of the world. The Valley's consistent contribution to the world's intellectual capital, combined with its regained industrial strength and international competitiveness, have given it something that a decade ago seemed like a delusional pipe-dream: yes, the Valley has a trade surplus. This means that Rich's government is no longer reliant on foreign investors to fund its deficit spending. Unfortunately the government has been unable to reign in its spending habits. Entitlement spending is still big and Rich just cannot say goodbye to his military. But the trade surplus, combined with the Valleyians increased

185

tendency to save slightly more than nothing, means that Rich can do what the Island did for decades and rely completely on domestic sources to fund his deficit spending. He and Banksy 'borrow' from the pension funds, the industrial complex and the banks. They go ever deeper into debt, but are able to borrow at low interest rates. Many states try to avoid paying any taxes to Rich, and there is constant talk of cessation. But ultimately the Valley does not split up and remains a political and fiscal union.

The Crimo continues to gain in strength. With their ever-growing buying power and their citizens' ever increasing demands, the Crimsons become the world's biggest spenders and soon the Crimo is the world's most traded currency, and over time it is clear that it has become the world's reserve.

Then comes the day that the Crimson economy overtakes their own. After the Crimson's first inflatable cat gets shot down by the Vodka Drinkers, they release another one that blows out to sea. Valleyian satellites immediately spot the large object – even on radar images it shows up as a cat. At first the cat gets sucked into a westerly and then into a polar easterly where it's blown violently off course. But then it gets sucked back into a major jet-stream and it's obvious that the cat is headed for the Valley. Word spreads and ambitious young Valleyians decide that this is their moment to shine. It is obvious that Crimsons love nothing more than cats. With all the big Crimson corporations in the Valley, there are plenty of Crimsons to sell things to, and word gets out that on the day the big cat arrives there will be a huge party. The Crimsons will be spending lots of money and of course, it makes sense that they will all want to buy decorative cats to commemorate the occasion. Valleyians get busy trying to predict when the cat will arrive. They call this operation Cat Arrival Time (CAT).

Although the cat is on course to blow over the Valley, CAT is not precisely known. Two organizations are set up to monitor the cat's movement. One is called Cat Arrival Time Association (CAT-A), the other is called Cat Arrival Time Bureau (CAT-B). CAT-A and CAT-B use different methods to calculate CAT. Their two times are averaged out to get CAT Calculated time, (CAT-C). Soon everyone in the Valley is talking about CATs A, B and C. Before long the bankers on Banksy Street are on board. They design products to give investors exposure to CAT, and with all the interest in the arrival, they start to feel important again. Investors can take out various positions regarding CAT. If you believe that the cat will arrive on CAT-C, then you are on CAT. If you believe it will arrive late, you are long CAT, and if you think it will arrive early, you are short CAT. They design products to give investors leveraged exposure to CAT, and soon CAT derivatives and securities can be used as collateral to take out loans. Soon FUCU bankers and Island Bankers get onboard and start buying up CAT derivatives and CAT securities. Banksy Street is booming again and the bankers are living large. But the GPBB is still fresh in their memories and in order to cover the multiple positions they've taken out, banks start issuing Credit Absence Transfers (CATs). They start to sell CATs to buyers of CAT derivatives and CAT securities. These offer protection in the instance that one's trading partner fails to pay out.

CAT related products have now become essential to the running of the economy, much like SPDs were back in their day. To protect themselves banks and large CAT buyers start taking out Catastrophe bonds known as CATs. Large insurers issue CAT specific Catastrophe bonds known as CAT CATs.

Financial engineers on Banksy Street and their equivalents around the world have, over the past decade, developed complex computer systems that analyze vast quantities of data and execute automated trades. This form of trading is known as algorithmic trading, or simply algo-trading. The algorithms analyze, amongst other things, weather patterns and keywords in news streams. With so much focus on CATs, algo-trading programmers have their hands full. The word CAT appears in so many different articles, and different usages of CAT should trigger different responses: buy, sell, hold, leverage, etc. But the programmers are smart, and things seem to be going well. Everyone is making money and everyone's eyes are on the big cat blowing towards the Valley from Crimson Land.

But then the cat passes over the E-FUCU border and the SHOOT computers mistake it for a Carpetmaker bomb and shoot it down. Chaos ensues.

CAT-A, CAT-B and CAT-C are all wrong. None took complete destruction into account. Those who are long CAT, short CAT and on CAT all stand to lose their money and CAT derivative and CAT securities holders begin to panic. CATs and CAT CATs are automatically triggered. The word CAT is now being read by every algo-trading program in the world. Programs cannot distinguish between buy-CAT sell-CAT hold-CAT and leverage-CAT commands. Conflicting messages are sent backwards and forwards, overwhelming computer systems. A popular journalist refers to the situation as the calamitous and terrible cat arrival time (CAT) catastrophe and tragedy. A program recently released by an avid follower of the Literal School of Acronymology scours all available data and forms automated acronyms. The acronym it forms for this article is CATCATCAT. This is the final straw. Algo-trading programs across the world

188

completely melt down, and back-up programs take over. Large banks and insurers had feared that one day something like this might happen and they have taken out Catastrophic Catastrophe Bonds, CAT CATs. At the height of the CAT market they adjusted these products slightly and issued CAT CAT CATs. The CATCATCAT causes the backup programs to automatically issue CAT CAT CATs. A popular online paper runs with the headline, 'CATCATCAT triggers CAT CAT CAT'. Some algo-trading rooms burst into flames. These fires cause the back-up back-up programs to take over. They automatically issue Catastrophically Catastrophic Catastrophe Bonds. Issuers of course had designed such bonds specifically for CATs – they are known as CAT CAT CAT CATs. The only place the insurers could save such vast sums of money was in Valleyian Bonds, and so finally the bond crisis begins. A headline reads CAT CAT CAT CATs triggered by CAT CAT CAT triggered CATCATCAT triggers Valley Bond Crisis.

Billions and Trillions of dollars start fleeing the bond market. But of course there is nowhere for all this money to go. At least, that is what everyone had assumed. But as it happens, a feral camel trapper, David "Davo" Stainbourn, who lives in Bruce Kingdom had recently decided to list his company on a small stock exchange. His company is really nothing more than a niche market, camel pelt tarpaulin supplier that he runs in the outback. But since he was a boy he had dreamed of turning the business his father founded into a public company, and so registered to list it in an initial public offering (IPO) under the name Camel-skin Tarpaulins. He was given the ticker symbol CAT. At the height of the crisis, back-up back-up systems override traders' manual operations. All the money in the world flows via exchanges and networks that allow massive off-market movements – dark pools – into Davo's pre-IPO company.

Tragically, Davo never knows he has all the money in the world. His company's IPO is automatically cancelled after he's killed in one of his own camel traps that same day, leaving neither heir nor will.

AFTERWORD

This is where the story ends. Beyond this, we know nothing. We have simply undertaken to interpret it as accurately as possible. After completing our task to the best of our abilities, we handed over the original parchments to a local museum in Yamaguchi Prefecture, Japan. Information about the museum can be found on our website. We welcome your thoughts and ideas. We do not wish to give away too much at this present moment. All we can say is that we have found more parchments in the area, and are currently working on interpreting them. The task is complex and arduous, but we believe that what we have uncovered may be of lasting importance. If you enjoyed what you have read here, we ask that you spread the word about the Yamaguchi Manuscripts. Both hardcopy and ebook versions are available on our website.

www.valleyeconomics.com

APPENDIX I
ACRONYMOLOGY

An acronym is an abbreviation formed from the initial components in a phrase or word. While many think it simple to form one, in reality it is not. The impact an acronym has on one can vary greatly. While some will still try to piece together their own acronyms, often with disastrous consequences, most acquire the services of an Acronymologist. Their services do not come cheap but usually assure the desired message is communicated. There are three main schools of acronymology: the Literal school, the Classical school (which is further divided into the Neoclassical school) and the Ironical school. The practitioners and advocates of the three main schools are extremely parochial and defend their schools and theories with great vigor.

The Literal School

Arguably the most widely practiced school and also the oldest. It is not known who founded this school but it is thought to have come into use as human's attention spans have became shorter and shorter. One of the early extremist Literal theorists had a vision of a time where all written words would be reduced to single letter capitalizations and numbers. He gave an example of a commonly expressed sentence. *'Are you meeting me tonight? See you.'* Under his system the sentence would appear *'R-U-MTNG-ME-2NIT? C-U'*. However most mainstream acronymologists and linguists alike believe it is highly improbable that the human written language would degenerate to such a degree.

The mechanical process of acronym formation in the literal school is very simple. The emphasis is on taking pre-formed phrases and simply replacing the first letters with Capitals. One important rule however is that the same word must not appear twice. It is said that this would debase the acronym. Whether the word is pronounceable in the native language or not matters little to the Literal acrynomologist. In fact later practitioners actually advocated having unpronounceable names. They cited studies showing that the process of irregular lip and tongue formation actually stimulates an area of the brain called the Cerebral-jargonus – the part associated with making things sound official.

To demonstrate the simple elegance of the Literal style an example is given below:

The local city is opening a new public college in a poor inner city area of The Valley capital called 'the "Stinky" Straights'. The literal acronymologist might simply use the graceful acronym SSPC – Stinky Straights Public College.

The Classical School

In modern times the Classical and Neo-classical schools are by far the most widely used. They are based on the concept of creating the acronym first and then finding the words to fit. Typically, good scrabble players make for talented Classical acronymologists.

Following the previous example, the Classical school practitioner could choose a name for the acronym first, say PICNIC and then arrange the words to make a relevant sentence – Public Inner City Noted Institution and College. Some also call this 'reverse acronymology'

For a Neo-classical acronymologist this is not striking enough and they would surely insist that the name inspire more awe. They would choose an acronym such as SCORE, and an equally inspiring name - Straights College Of Rich Education.

The Ironical School

The newest of the three schools, the Ironical school is based on one of either two principles: creating an acronym that states the obvious, or one that points out an inherent flaw in the system it describes. It is thought that by appearing honest and straightforward the acronym is more believable and hence people will have greater respect for the institution or subject described by the acronym. This is possibly the hardest of the three schools to master because the acronymologist must have a thorough understanding of the subject material – often more than those who obtain the acronymologists services. These extremely highly paid practitioners often move into the field of acronymology after first specializing in another field. Economic acronymologists are rumored to be the most highly paid professionals outside of investment bankers.

An example again using the aforementioned situation might be: NOSTUDI – Newly Opened Straights Teaching Under Direct Instruction. The irony of such an acronym can clearly be seen and it is sure to garner appreciation.

ABBREVIATIONS

3S	Stainbourn Strategic Services
ADs	Austerity days
ASSD	Animal skin shelter device
BAIF	Business and Investor Friendly States
BBL	Big Big Leader
CAT	Cat Arrival Time
CAT	Camel-skin Tarpaulins
CAT	Credit Absence Transfer
CAT-A	Cat arrival time Association
CAT-B	Cat arrival time Bureau
CAT-C	CAT Calculated time
CATs	Catastrophe bonds
CAT CATs	CAT Catastrophe bonds
CATCATCATs	CAT Catastrophic Catastrophe bonds
CATCATCATCATs	CAT Catastrophically Catastrophic Catastrophe bonds
CSET	Cheesemakers School of Economic Theory
DAMN	Disastrous Aftermath Madness Nuisance
DIM	Digital inflation machine
Downubaiku*	Downgrade bike man
DUMFUC	Dairy Union Monetary but not Fiscal Union Congress
DW1	Devaluation wars 1
EA	Economic Armageddon

E-FUCU	Eastern Fiscal Union Currency United
FUCU	Fiscal Union Currency United
IGCMA	International gold chain makers award
IM	Inflation machine
LBC s	Lying banker calculations
MMA	Meow Meow Agent
MM War	Mighty Mighty War
MUFM	Mint Used For Minting
NIEM	New Improved Economic Measurement
NOSP	Note Skim and Prick
NUT	New Up Town
NVST	Northern School Valley Theorist
PTD	Primitus Tony Declaration
PWOS-NOM-FOR	Post War Official System with No Official Mechanism For Official Revaluation
RGs	Rich's Goons
RTH	Regina the horrible
SHOOT	Strategic Hotspot On Open Terrain
SHOOTAMAN	SHOOT Alliance Mutual Agreement Non-Treaty
SOIK	Spate of inflation killings
TULSOA	The Ultimate Literal School of Acronymology
VIC	Valley-Island-Cheesemakers
VICABC	Valley-Island-Cheesemakers Annual Bankers' Convention
VIEW-A-HOT-P	Vast Impressive Extraordinary Wonderful Amazing Hall Of The People

GLOSSARY

AAA	The highest rated investment grade security.
Alan & Alan	A ratings agency.
ASSD	A free-standing shelter made of animal skins.
Austerity days	A period of austerity.
Banksy Street	The main financial district of The Valley named after the first financial innovator, Banksy the First.
Biggest Cat	An unofficial Crimson anthem written by the BBL's wife. A pop-rendition was later released to international acclaim.
Black Panther Holdings	The name of a defunct investment bank.
Carpetmakers	An ancient oil rich country
Cheesemakers	A nation famous for their precisely manufactured goods and cheese.
Credit Absence Transfer	A derivative that enables an entity to hedge against default of a financial product
Crimo	The currency of the Crimsons.
Crimson Land	A vast resource rich country with a large population (recently overtaken the Valley as the largest economy in the world)

CSET	A distinct school of economic theory that advocates free markets and honest money
Csetian	Adjective of CSET
DAMN	The after-effects of the great dam collapse.
DUMFUCS	Pre Homerstandt crisis name for countries using the Daiso currency unit.
death by cheese	Method of capital punishment whereby a person is strapped to a large wheel of hard cheese and rolled off a high cliff (early versions using soft cheese were often partially ineffective and deemed inhumane).
death by burning	The preferred method of execution in Crimson Land.
debt induced doldrums	A state of relative depression due to the abuse of debt.
devaluing wars	Series of world-wide currency devaluations
digital inflation machine	Inflation machine which is connected via high speed internet to a central bank.
Downubaiku *	Downgrade bike man (a man who downgrades from a car to a bike)
downubiku-famu-helpu	A man who downgrades from a car to a bike to get money to help his family
dung Standard	The unsuccessful attempt to create an official money standard using manure.

FUCU	Revised Name for countries using the Daiso currency.
Gouder	The currency of The Cheesemakers.
inflation machine	A device, usually rotated by hand, to keep prices updated in extreme inflationary environments.
Hor. Regina	A mis-struck slogan on a Vim gold coin commonly known to mean Regina the Horrible.
Isle	The currency of the Island
LBCs	Created by the Lyst brothers, it determines, through statistical analysis, the likelihood of a banker lying in any verbal transaction. It can also be used in determining the moral trends of a financial system as a whole. It has been used as the underlying asset for derivatives.
Mighty Mighty War	The most destructive and horrific war of modern times involving the whole world.
MUFM	The official name given to the Cheesemaker national mint.
Note Skim & Prick	Central bankers' alliance aimed at suppressing the price of gold.
NSVT	A distinct school of economic theory that advocates government intervention to reinvigorate an economy
POWER	The large scale reforms undertaken to modernize Crimson Land's economy.

POTI-effect	Using advanced financial accounting techniques (computers or wheelbarrows) to keep a currency undervalued.
PTD	An agreement to go off the gold standard and devalue the Isle.
PWOS-NOM-FOR	A defunct currency system involving a pegged Vim gold standard.
Rex Rich Tortoreous	The slogan on the first gold Vim meaning *King Rich The Torturer*
rice-eater	A derogatory term initially used to insult the Stainbourn family but now used for any unsuccessful and/or unlucky person
Sharpe-Prick derivative	An investment-grade security backed by a pool of loans.
Sharpe-Prick Bank	A non-bank, bank specializing in mortgage lending.
SOIK	Random inflation related killings often involving inflation machines.
Stagu-depu-re	Stagflationary depression
STAMO26A3	The recessive gene (Stainbourn Moron–26–member 3) responsible for a lack of common sense and extreme overconfidence in humans.
Theftian	A minority group originating in the northern region of The Valley.
tier II capital	Gold teeth.
TULOSA	The most well respected acronym creation institution in the world.
Valley	An ancient resource laden country located in a temperate region.

Valleyian	The adjective used for people from the country named the Valley.
VIC	The name of a pact involving three nations.
VICABC	The annual central bankers convention involving the VIC nations.
Ventak	A distinct ethnic group from the Valley the majority of whom worship the supreme deity Mr. Tak.
Vician	A person from one of the VIC countries
Vim	The currency of The Valley.
Vodka Drinkers Country	A vast country that has many natural resources. The only country in which all citizens consume vodka throughout the day.
Whack-em-Crack-em	A form of coal seam gas extraction.
WOLF News	A Valleyian nationalistic right leaning news network
XXX	The lowest possible rating for an investment product/in default.

*Variations in common usage:

Downubiku-famu-helpu-no-appro – a man who downgrades from a car to a bike to help his family but still gets no appreciation from his mother in law.

Downubiku-famu-helpu-no-appro-throwu-trainu – as above, but cannot handle the situation and throws himself in front of a train.